# Ride the *Ark* Through *Armageddon*

# Ride the Ark Through Armageddon

A Survival Guide for Mankind

# RICHARD B. KELSEY

A Division of WINEPRESS PUBLISHING

© 2006 by Richard Kelsey. All rights reserved.

Printed in the United States of America

Packaged by Pleasant Word, a division of WinePress Publishing, P.O. Box 428, Enumclaw, WA 98022. The views expressed or implied in this work do not necessarily reflect those of Pleasant Word, a division of WinePress Publishing. Ultimate design, content, and editorial accuracy of this work are the responsibilities of the author.

No part of this publication may be reproduced, stored in a retrieval system, or transmitted in any way by any means—electronic, mechanical, photocopy, recording, or otherwise—without the prior permission of the copyright holder, except as provided by U.S. copyright law.

Unless otherwise noted, all Scriptures are taken from the Holy Bible, New International Version, Copyright © 1973, 1978, 1984 by the International Bible Society. Used by permission of Zondervan Publishing House. The "NIV" and "New International Version" trademarks are registered in the United States Patent and Trademark Office by the International Bible Society.

ISBN 1-57921-526-2
Library of Congress Catalog Card Number: 2002115819

To everyone who has a
strong love for the truth

# CONTENTS

About This Book ........................................................................9
Acknowledgments ...................................................................11
Introduction ............................................................................12

1. The Mortgage of the Earth to Satan ..................................13
2. My People, Enter Your Rooms............................................21
3. The Invitation to the Great Banquet ..................................31
4. Seals and Horses.................................................................41
5. The Midnight Hour ............................................................57
6. Trumpets—Sounding of Judgment ....................................67
7. An Invasion of Locusts ......................................................81
8. The Final Woe ....................................................................91
9. Deception Is on the Horizon............................................107
10. The Overcoming Church in Prophecy .............................119
11. Choose Your Battles Carefully .........................................127
12. Paradise Restored .............................................................137
13. The Feast Days—Now and Then .....................................147
14. Lampstands, Olive Trees, and Witnesses.........................157
15. The Woman and Her Offspring .......................................165
16. 144,000 of the Tribes of Israel .........................................177

17. The Great Disappointment ..................................................187
18. Through the Door and into His Image..............................201

End Notes ....................................................................................207

*Additional information can be found at the author's website:*
*Richkelsey.org*

# ABOUT THIS BOOK

**I Have Been to the Mountaintop**

In 1995 I had a vision concerning aspects of Revelation's meaning. Jesus Christ taught me about a mystery in Revelation, and he asked me to tell the world about it. An invisible heavenly hand was placed upon my head and I felt knowledge enter in. I heard a voice command me to, "Write a book."

This visitation and the knowledge that was imparted significantly changed the way I understood Revelation. My eyes were opened, and as I pored over the Scriptures right after that heavenly visitation I was led by the Spirit of God to finally understand the great mystery hidden within Revelation's pages. This mystery and its meaning is spelled out in this book.

The crux of *Ride the Ark Through Armageddon* is the explanation of end-time Bible prophecy, including a breakdown of each of Revelation's plagues—the horses, the seals, the trumpets and the bowl plagues. This book also goes into detail concerning the timing of the pre-wrath catching up of believers—the Rapture—and how this event is woven into Revelation's time-frame.

I demonstrate that much of the popular views concerning Revelation's plagues and the time-lines taught today lack credibility. Understanding the symbolism within Revelation's pages is essential so that we can prepare for the coming hour. Without the light of truth, it will be impossible for some to see through the coming darkness.

However, *Ride the Ark Through Armageddon* is not just about Bible prophecy, it's about hope, faith, and dreams. Not unrealistic dreams, or a hope that can not be fulfilled, but the sure hope we have in Jesus Christ of eternal life, and the sure dream we all share of living forever in paradise.

This book tells a story; starting off in the Garden of Eden with the fall of man, then covering the days of Noah with the great flood and the ark carrying away God's elect. It explains how that flood was an illustration of God's wrath at the end of this age and how that ark was a natural counterpart to a spiritual design.

Scriptures are explained in a way that makes sense. Teaching is put together in a manner that builds faith, without having to rely on blind faith in order to believe.

I see and interpret the symbolism within Revelation's pages by comparing its prophecies to prophecies found elsewhere in the Bible, bringing forth a realistic picture of future events. For example: in Chapter Eight of Revelation we see "something like a huge mountain, all ablaze, was thrown into the sea." Instead of looking at this prophecy as representing a literal object hitting Earth's oceans I explain the mountain's symbolic application.

Mountains elsewhere in the Bible including Revelation are symbolic of world government. So I teach that the "mountain all ablaze" is symbolizing a world government impacting the nations. Speaking on the same subject it's written in Jeremiah "I am against you, O destroying mountain, you who destroy the whole earth,' declares the LORD. 'I will stretch out my hand against you, roll you off the cliffs, and make you a burned-out mountain'" (Jer. 51:25).

The mountain that God rolled off the cliffs—presumably into the sea—in time past was the Babylonian Empire. The same language used in Jeremiah illustrating how Babylon of old would be destroyed is also used in Revelation concerning modern Babylon's coming destruction.

Ancient Babylon did fall and its mountain burned out just as prophesied—God did cast its burning mountain into the sea, figuratively speaking. However, at that time, no one on earth saw a literal mountain descend into the ocean; that wasn't necessary to fulfill Bible prophecy back then. Likewise, I conclude that, in the days ahead, no one will see a literal mountain cast into the sea as our prophecy in Revelation is fulfilled.

If what I have recorded in this work is true then many who are looking for a literal fulfillment to Revelation's prophecies could be deceived. If what this book says is false then it will be obvious to all as Revelation's plagues befall mankind.

In this work Revelation's prophecies are portrayed as unseen forces waging battle in invisible realms, with this battle spilling over from the spirit world into our streets.

# ACKNOWLEDGMENTS

For editing and guiding the book's content:

Sally E. Stuart—Author of 29 books, including the annual (Christian Writers Market Guide)
Susan Titus Osborne—(The Christian Communicator)
Barbara A. Robidoux—(The Christian Communicator)
Judi Wu—PREP Publishing

# INTRODUCTION

This creation was marred by the transgression of angelic spirits who helped plunge mankind into the darkness of sin. Looking at the world with this understanding explains many things, like why evil is all around us and why the Creator seems so hard to find. The Almighty has allowed us this rare display of lawlessness both to teach us and as a tool to ensnare and separate the disobedient. Before His eternal kingdom comes, the dross must be removed.

Chapter 1

# THE MORTGAGE OF THE EARTH TO SATAN

In the glorious days when God created the earth, "all the angels shouted for joy."¹ The *Spirit of God*² hovered over this world like a loving mother hen over her young. God saved His most precious creation for last: He made man from the dust of the earth and woman from man. He set them in a beautiful garden with no threat of anything to hurt them. The temperature didn't get too cold at night, and instead of rain,³ heavy dew covered the ground every morning—Adam and Eve were living in Paradise. God visited them in the garden in the cool of the day. We can only imagine what a wonderful relationship they were building.

God told Adam to "be fruitful and increase in number; fill the earth and subdue it"⁴—in other words, to have children and dominate the planet. But Adam was also in paradise to learn. He and his wife were there to be shaped into the image and likeness of God. Just as a man desires his wife to become of the same mind, to trust and cherish him, God was looking for such a companion in mankind.

The Creator had every good intention toward His children. Mankind was given an awesome opportunity. The only rule that God laid down in all of paradise was "You must not eat from the tree of the knowledge of good and evil" (Gen. 2:17). Day by day, Adam and Eve grew in wisdom and knowledge. They were maturing, learning about life, and developing character. They grew to know and love each other.

## Satan's Folly

The Scriptures record this about Satan: "You were blameless in your ways from the day you were created till wickedness was found in you" (Ezek. 28:15). The word *wickedness* literally means "lawlessness." Satan violated God's laws. Before his disobedience, he was called Lucifer. The word *Lucifer* has beautiful connotations; it means "morning star" (Isa. 14:12). He was "the bright and shining one."

Lucifer may have been in existence long before earth was created, standing in an exalted position before the courts of the Most High. One day among countless days, this unblemished entity carefully considered the order of things in heaven. He wondered about the Creator's code of right and wrong. Curiosity began to rule in Lucifer's mind, and he may have been thinking, "I wonder what it would be like if only things were different?" He was obsessed with what was happening on earth. Lucifer came to understand that God, who dispenses justice and judgment without bias,[5] was to give his mature sons and daughters the reward of their own[6] merit. He came to the startling realization that one day, men and women would be exalted in position above him.

Envision Lucifer in heaven, pacing back and forth, brainstorming, thinking about how to maintain his position at the center of God's creation and to restrain mankind to a lower level. He began masterminding how to bring God's children out of divine favor. Pride became a factor in his decision making. Lucifer was in heaven, in glory, yet he was never tried in the fires of temptation and tested in the day of adversity like mankind would be. He had never learned the virtues of trusting God.

Before his transgression, it was written of him, "You were anointed as a guardian cherub, for so I ordained you" (Ezek. 28:14). God had appointed Lucifer and all the angels[7] to protect men. Angels were to watch over people to keep them out of harm's way. The more Lucifer thought about his own standing and the ultimate position of mankind, the more he became depressed. Since he was perfect in beauty, in his mind he was the one to be admired among God's creation, not lowly man. The thought of Adam and Eve being exalted above him seemed unbearable. Satan determined to prevent their exaltation. So he set a trap. The word *Satan* means "to ambush in quiet" as one patiently lies in wait for his prey. Satan is also called the *devil*, which means "to pierce through" as with a weapon.

The devil, haunted by his own pride, questioned God's supremacy. Satan in his heart said: "I will raise my throne above the stars of God . . . I will make myself like the Most High" (Isa. 14:13, 14). He started to hate God. Imagine that! The very God of love, Satan learned to hate.

Satan threw caution to the wind. This sly devil deceived many of the angels. Then he set his sights on mankind. If he could get people to display the same distrust in God that he did, this might overthrow God's authority. Satan could then become "the god of this age" (2 Corinthians 4:4).

## The Fall of Man

Satan waited in paradise for the perfect moment to strike. Adam was away from Eve, unaware that his wife was in trouble. Eve was probably gazing at the fruit on that mysterious tree from which her husband told her not to eat when a serpent spoke to her.

"Now the serpent was more crafty than any of the wild animals the Lord God had made" (Gen. 3:1). If the devil had spoken through a seething red dragon with horns on its head,[8] he probably would have alarmed Eve. But no, the devil wanted to make Eve comfortable. So he spoke to her through a beautiful serpent. He said to the woman, "Did God really say, 'You must not eat from any tree in the garden'?" (Gen. 3:1). Eve answered:

> We may eat fruit from the trees in the garden, But God did say "You must not eat fruit from the tree that is in the middle of the garden, and you must not touch it, or you will die." (Gen. 3:2b–3)

Then Satan brought out the hook. He said:

> You will not surely die. For God knows that when you eat of it your eyes will be opened, and you will be like God, knowing good and evil. (Gen. 3:4–5)

The devil made the false claim that Eve would be like God if only she disobeyed His command. Satan alleged that God was holding Eve back from her true glory so He could dominate her. Satan convinced Eve that the God of love did not have her best interests in mind. If Eve had thought about the serpent's question logically, she might have had doubts. Why was this lowly creature[9] instructing her? She could have answered the serpent, "Let me talk it over with my husband first." After all, the tree wasn't going anywhere.

Instead, she got caught up by the serpent's charm and took a drastic leap of faith in what he said.[10] She took the fruit and swallowed the bait. She bought into Satan's scheme, and her eyes were opened. The devil had approached the one with the least knowledge, and Eve got swindled. She didn't get what Satan promised her; she lost everything! However, Satan was on his way to fulfilling his dream.

Do you know why the devil approached Eve and not Adam? Because Adam had a stronger relationship with God than Eve did. It was Adam[11] whom God instructed how to manage paradise, what fruit to eat and what not. That was secondhand information to Eve, but Adam had heard it straight from God. Eve didn't have all her facts straight when she argued her case with the serpent. God had not told Adam he would die if he touched the fruit.

Now came the real challenge: if Adam would also question the Creator's laws and violate his Father's only rule, then he, too, would disobey God's instructions. God had told Adam to subdue and conquer the earth, to take possession of it, and to stand as ruler. Adam was the Father's firstborn human son, and he would hold the birthright,[12] the deed to the planet. This deed is what Satan was after.

## Adam, Why Did You Do It?

What possible motive would cause Adam to disobey God? The Scriptures clearly indicate, "Adam was not the one deceived; it was the woman who was deceived" (1 Tim. 2:14). Therefore, we can't maintain that Satan or Eve deceived Adam. Why in the world would Adam eat the forbidden fruit? The answer is in Gen. 3:12: "The man said, 'The woman you put here with me—she gave me some fruit from the tree, and I ate it.'" If Eve had lied to Adam and he had believed the lie, then he would have been deceived. However, the Scripture cannot be ignored. Let's think for a moment. We know Eve gave Adam the fruit, but if she didn't deceive Adam, then how did she convince him to eat it?

Envision Eve with the fruit still in her hand, the juice dripping down her chin, waiting to become like God, closing her eyes in anxious expectation only to hear the serpent's mocking laughter. Envision Eve falling to the ground, weeping, shivering in terror as the full impact of the situation hit her. Think about the grief Eve was suffering. Consider the magnitude of anguish her soul was going through. She was scared and became desperate. She knew the moment her eyes were opened that she was now different from her husband. She had a full understanding of the mess she was in.

Picture loving Adam coming back to the garden after exploring the surrounding terrain only to find Eve in an emotional fit. Think about the grief that Adam faced when he realized God would separate the two of them. When Eve tearfully looked Adam in the face, asking him not to abandon her to God's judgment, giving him the fruit, and begging him to eat it,[13] Adam was faced with a decision. Adam chose to side with the one he loved the most. Unfortunately, Adam loved Eve more than God.

Keep in mind that neither Satan nor the foolish angels[14] nor Adam fully understood the roles they were playing. Adam played right into the devil's scheme. He reinforced the idea that God cannot be trusted because Adam did not trust God with the fate of his wife's soul.

## Adam Turned His Back on God

Having abandoned his faith in God's discretion, Adam set out to keep his wife from dealing with God all by herself. He took the fruit from the woman's hand and ate it. Suddenly his eyes were opened, and he realized the full tragedy of his situation. This was a dark moment in the history of mankind.

Satan had put before Adam, the head of the Father's creation, circumstances that caused him to exhibit distrust in the Creator. Satan won! Our original parents trusted the devil and his ways over those of a holy God. The devil forced open a trial when he got man to follow his lead in transgressing God's laws, and the devil got his due. God granted an appointed time[15] for Satan to govern the earth; this season is actually a great benefit in our maturing process. Now all creation understands that a world where evil is allowed is a world filled with violence, lies, anguish, sorrow, and death. What a stark contrast to the paradise God originally provided for us in which to learn!

Eve had never heard a lie before the father of lies showed up at her door. People were not created to die. Nothing was to be hurt on God's holy mountain. Oh, how things have changed! The devil is ruling the world. Does that mean God is a victim? No, it means the devil, the foolish angels, and those who follow Satan to the pit[16] are victims of their own making. In this world, we fashion ourselves either to God's glory or after our own lusts.

If it weren't for Lucifer's fall and the fall of man that followed, all creation never would have seen this grand display of evil. Wise people who can see the snare of evil lying in wait for the scornful have a wonderful opportunity. They can choose to submit to God and practice holiness in an evil world. With their faith tested by the devil, the rewards will be much greater than if Adam and Eve had never fallen.

However, all this evil needs to come to an end. Although the end sometimes justifies the means, in this case, the means are unacceptable. Judgment must be recompensed for the righteous. A loving Father should stop this, right? Yes, but due legal process must be followed in order for this conflict to go down in the records as being won fairly.

Satan gained "the power of death"[17] over man. He also gained the position[18] Adam held. Adam forfeited his right to subdue the earth when he made the decision to follow Eve in the transgression. Now Adam was no longer the dominant one—the devil was. The devil had mankind and many foolish angels backing him[19] in this insurrection; therefore the earth was delivered into his hand for a season. Forcing men and angels to comply with God's program was out of the question. The devil won the right to rule hands down. God, being fair, is now watching from the sidelines. Yet he is not far from any one of us.

After the fall, God drove mankind from Paradise. Satan was given great authority over this creation. With the curse in effect, death began its reign. If we have trouble understanding this, one look at what happened in the following three chapters of Genesis confirms this premise: "The LORD saw how great man's wickedness on the earth had become, and that every inclination of the thoughts of his heart was only evil all the time" (Gen. 6:5).

Mankind soon became so corrupt that God sent a great flood to remove them from the face of the earth. Only Noah and his family who went into the Ark survived to see the post-flood earth cleansed from that evil generation. However, even those eight who were saved possessed fallen natures. To this day, the human race is still a far cry from the state God intended and called us to in the Garden.

What about the Almighty Creator and His quest for children to be made into His image? "The creation waits in eager expectation for the sons of God to be revealed" (Rom. 8:19). Isn't this what earth was created for, so God could raise sons and daughters to maturity? The answer is "yes." However, God is just. Instead of stopping the devil's insurrection, He is using it to teach us.

God's original plan—to raise men to maturity and let them trust and love Him out of free will, then to reward the good with His glory—is still being fulfilled. But it takes effort to go against the winds of adversity. Few people exert that kind of integrity. Those who do, God will not forsake. Our Father is still waiting for the harvest of His children.

Therefore, God worked with fallen man and brought about a system of ordinances for the children who loved Him; these individuals would reject the devil and his ways.

## The Sacrificial Lamb

The main ordinance our Father put into action was the lamb sacrifice. For man to escape the wrath brought about by the transgression of God's laws, the sacrifice of a lamb was implemented. Those who laid hands on these lambs, imputing their sins to the animals in a symbolic act of faith, then offering those lambs up to God in sacrifice, were counted worthy to receive the true Lamb of God—Jesus Christ—whose offering[20] would be manifest in due time.

# Chapter 2

# MY PEOPLE, ENTER YOUR ROOMS

This earth, as it nears the midnight hour, is in a conflict with God. On this planet and in the heavens above, a spiritual battle is unfolding. One day this war will pierce through the invisible realm of the spirit and fill our streets with the slain.

The Bible does not record how long Adam and Eve lived before they were driven from Paradise due to the transgression. However, we can be certain that the first conflict between God and Satan, and between good and evil, arose in the heavens. Then, because of Satan's interaction with mankind, it spread into our earthly realm like a dark plague. This evil brought in the curse and death from the hand of Almighty God, for God cannot allow evil to remain unchecked. Therefore the Lord and the armies of heaven are waiting for a day to bring this transgression to an end. "In that day the LORD will punish the powers in the heavens above and the kings on the earth below. They will be herded together like prisoners bound in a dungeon; they will be shut up in prison and be punished after many days" (Isa. 24:21–22). In the recesses of this abyss,[21] Satan shall be looked upon narrowly.

As sons and daughters were born unto Adam and Eve, wickedness, corruption, violence, and death began to reign in the earth. Few people in the generation that followed Adam had the spiritual fortitude to abide in the plan of redemption the Almighty set forth.

Mankind fell into perverse wickedness. It was because of man's sinfulness that the Lord set out to destroy him from the face of the earth. However, there were a few righteous among the wicked—the Lord used Noah as a testimony of His grace. Noah, through a divine calling, preached salvation and deliverance from divine judgment. Through the ministry of this prophet, God laid out a welcome mat the size of a ship and provided a door for men to enter. God provided safe haven for those who would heed the call. He gave that generation time and opportunity to enter the Ark. When they failed to heed the cry of Noah, the Lord shut in his elect and rained down judgment upon the unbelieving.

A similar judgment befell Sodom and Gomorrah. These twin cities were corrupt and had forsaken the holy covenant. God did not punish those cities without notice. He sent out callers to warn the righteous. His angels beckoned the people to flee before the plague of fire and brimstone destroyed their cities. Yet for the most part, the people would not hear.

So shall it be in our generation. Once again, callers will go forth at the midnight hour, sent from God with a divine welcome, pointing to the ark of safety and faith in the Lamb of God. Yet many of the people shall not hear, for the Lord has given them ears dull of hearing because of their sinfulness. They will also close their eyes to the truth, and the perverseness of their hearts will kindle the fury of God's wrath. Therefore the Lord will pour out the bowls of trembling spoken of in Revelation. The dregs from the bowls of the Lamb's wrath will fall like rain on the children of disobedience: "The end will come like a flood."[22]

However, for the sake of God's elect,[23] an ark will sail over this troubled world. Once again, God will shut His people in, for the fruit is now ripe in the time of God's harvest, and the Lord of the harvest will come to reap from the vine. It's written: "The fig tree forms its early fruit; the blossoming vines spread their fragrance. Arise, come, my darling; my beautiful one, come with me. My dove in the clefts of the rock, in the hiding places on the mountainside, show me your face, let me hear your voice; for your voice is sweet, and your face is lovely" (Song of Sol. 2:13–14). The "hiding places on the mountainside" are an illustration of a place where Jesus will hide his bride (the church) in the days of his wrath.

## A Time of Distress Never to Be Equaled Again

"For then there shall be great distress, unequaled from the beginning of the world until now—and never to be equaled again" (Matt. 24:21). According to Scripture, this time of "great distress" that Christ spoke of encompasses the last plagues of Revelation, including the battle of Armageddon. Both the Old and New Testament Scriptures promise that God's elect will be spared from this abominable space of time—a time of judgment upon earth. This will be punishment upon the unbelieving[24] who have turned from the knowledge of God. Judgment will avenge[25] all the faithful throughout time whom evil men have cut down like grass—men and women who stood as God's anointed, preaching the Word of God when the winds of adversity raged.

Before the broom of God's final judgment sweeps throughout this earth, the Scriptures state that Christ will catch up his elect to keep them "from the hour of trial that is going to come upon the whole world to test those who live on the earth" (Rev. 3:10). For people to be kept from the very *hour* of affliction, it would seem they must be somewhere else when the clock bell tolls.

Jesus forecast distress upon nations. The waves of the sea shall roar. Men's hearts will fail them for fear. These are the days of vengeance, but not vengeance upon believers. We shall be kept from this hour. As the shadow of pain and darkness befalls this earth, once more an ark shall sail. We shall rise up on the wings of eagles. We shall "fly along like clouds, like doves to their nests" (Isa. 60:8).

## The Great Rapture Allegory

How many comprehend the great Rapture allegory found within the Bible? That is the ark that lifted Noah and his family above the earth while the judgment of God poured down. The great flood of Noah's time was a representation of the wrath of God, which will come upon the ungodly at the end of this age. The ark, as it was lifted above the earth, was a model of the coming ascension of God's people. In the Old Testament, there are illustrations of biblical concepts which parallel spiritual events in the New Testament.

A wooden ark floating above the earth with God's elect safely inside, sheltered from harm while the world is destroyed, certainly fits as a prophetic illustration depicting the Rapture. Also, the great rain, earthquakes, volcanoes, thunder, and lightning storms, followed by a massive increase of water upon the earth, certainly would fit as an illustration of the wrath to come as forecast in Revelation. In connection with his return, Jesus drew parallels to the days of Noah. Jesus is called the "Son of Man" many times in the Bible. In this next verse, Christ is referring to himself: "As it was in the days of Noah, so it will be at the coming of the Son of Man" (Matt. 24:37). Therefore, let's give this concept of the Old Testament ark depicting a catching away or Rapture of God's faithful a fair examination.

## In the Days of Noah

In Noah's day, mankind had become wicked: "So God said to Noah, 'I am going to put an end to all people, for the earth is filled with violence because of them. I am surely going to destroy both them and the earth . . . I am going to bring floodwaters on the earth to destroy all life under the heavens, every creature that has the breath of life in it. Everything on earth will perish'" (Gen. 6:13, 17). "But Noah found favor in the eyes of the LORD" (Gen. 6:8). In a time when most of mankind was living in gross sin, Noah was seeking God's direction and following in his paths.

## The Prophet and Ark Builder—Noah

This man of faith stood as a prophet pointing the way of deliverance to a disbelieving world. God commanded Noah to build an ark. Noah, along with his family, built the ark according to God's instructions. Surely throngs of people journeyed to see the ark as it was being built. Many of the curious would stay for a while and hear the old man's message about a coming flood. Noah surely poured out his heart, warning the crowds to repent from their wickedness and to enter the ark with him. He had heard from God; he knew his message was true; but to the multitudes, Noah was a man to be mocked. The people of Noah's day were too proud to be counted among his household.

## A Safe Haven

As the raging flood increased upon the face of the Earth, Noah and his family had entered their chambers inside. God made a covenant with Noah and those who entered with him, promising that he would keep them safe from the coming wrath. Noah never lost faith in the vision, and when all was ready, "the LORD shut him in" (Gen. 7:16). It's interesting to note that God shut the door of the natural ark.

Although only eight human souls went in, the masses finally believed in Noah's words. As the water was rising upon the earth, those outside the ark began to reflect on what Noah had preached. The torrential rain, earthquakes, thunder, and lightning bolts terrified them; it became obvious they were going to die. Undoubtedly, many ran to the ark, pounding desperately on the door, trying to enter as the heavy rain began. But they couldn't get in. God had sealed the door and it was too late for them. As the crowds watched from the hilltops, suffering, they saw the ark rise upon the churning waters. Many began to pray like they had never prayed before. Many repented of their sins—then they died.

## One Shall Be Taken and the Other Left

Jesus Christ spoke this parable: "For in the days before the flood, people were eating and drinking, marrying and giving in marriage, up to the day Noah entered the ark; and they knew nothing about what would happen until the flood came and took them all away. That is how it will be at the coming of the Son of Man. Two men will be in the field; one will be taken and the other left. Two women will be grinding with a hand mill; one will be taken and the other left" (Matt. 24:38–41). These verses show men and women being taken while others are left behind. They also depict people going up by using the ark as an example, for the ark was lifted up.

## Caught Up to Meet the Lord in the Air

"For the Lord himself will come down from heaven, with a loud command, with the voice of the archangel and with the trumpet call of God, and the dead in Christ will rise first. After that, we who are still alive and are left will be caught up together with them in the clouds to meet the Lord in the air. And so we will be with the Lord forever" (1 Thess. 4:16–17). These verses do not state that Jesus is stepping foot on earth. During this resurrection, it's penned that we are meeting the Lord in the air, adding weight to the prospect that we may rise above like Noah did to escape the coming distress. Please take note: a resurrection of the "dead in Christ" and also a reference to those "who are still alive" was mentioned in our text. A resurrection is also mentioned in the next text we will view.

## You Who Dwell in the Dust, Wake Up

> "But your dead will live; their bodies will rise. You who dwell in the dust, wake up and shout for joy. Your dew is like the dew of the morning; the earth will give birth to her dead. Go, my people, enter your rooms and shut the doors behind you; hide yourselves for a little while until his wrath has passed by. See, the Lord is coming out of his dwelling to punish the people of the earth for their sins. The earth will disclose the blood shed upon her; she will conceal her slain no longer." (Isa. 26:19–21)

Let's consider the phrase, "You who dwell in the dust, wake up and shout for joy." The Scriptures sometimes refer to people sleeping in death. The term "wake up" here in Isaiah is a reference to the awakening of the dead. "You who dwell in the dust" obviously indicates the condition of the dead before this resurrection; their bodies had literally turned to dust! The phrase, "Your dew is like the dew of the morning" has beautiful connotations; it's an illustration—a parable. In the early morning, dew covers the fields of this earth. When the sun appears in all of its glory, the dew rises. The sun represents[26] Jesus Christ; the dew rising is symbolic of the souls of men and women who are caught up.

This passage in Isaiah clearly shows a resurrection. It strongly implies Rapture by saying, "Hide yourselves for a little while until his wrath has passed by." Where is it that the resurrected, along with the living, go to hide until God's judgment on earth has ceased? The answer: Out of this world.

This pre-wrath resurrection[27] and Rapture in Isaiah is quite different from the second resurrection of the dead as found in Rev. 20:13, not only in time and place, but also in content and purpose.

## But Your Dead Will Live—Their Bodies Will Rise

Still referring to our text from Isaiah, let's consider the saying "their bodies will rise." The Hebrew word used for *rise* in the text means "lift up, rise up," or "stir up." In other passages from the Old Testament, this word has been used to describe one rising from sleep.

The word *wrath* in our text literally means "froth at the mouth," and it is used to show God's displeasure with sin. The text itself parallels this term, "wrath," with a time when the Lord will "punish the people of the earth for their sins" (Isa. 26:21). Could this time of punishment spoken of in Isaiah be the same as the great tribulation to come spoken of by Christ?

## Rooms in the Ark

God instructed the prophet Noah to make rooms in the ark (Gen. 6:14). Noah built rooms for his family and built stables for the animals. The Hebrew word used for the ark's rooms, *qen*, as recorded in Genesis, is a term that an architect would use to define a place of storage. This ship was simply a storage vessel so that life might be preserved upon earth. The old rugged ark did its job as designed.

Yet the material illustration of this Old Testament vessel palls in comparison to the glory of the New Testament sanctuary in which we will find shelter. For one thing, the first ark was made out of wood; the coming ark is made without hands.

With that in mind, let's look to Isaiah's prophecy again. "Go, my people, enter your rooms and shut the doors behind you; hide yourselves for a little while until his wrath has passed by" (Isa. 26:20). The Hebrew word used here for "rooms" is *cheder*. It has beautiful connotations. It means "inner chamber, innermost part, to enclose." The emphasis of this word is "inner." This word is referring to a deep place inside—a place of refuge.[28] The "inner chamber" we shall enter will be a glorious place, in the center of God's design for us. Yet this inner place also has a spiritual counterpart. God is asking His people to come into an inner sanctuary long before we ascend on high. "Go, my people, enter your rooms" has a figurative partial fulfillment here on earth.

# Chapter 3

# THE INVITATION TO THE GREAT BANQUET

The Greek word for "church" in the New Testament is *ekklesia*, which is derived from *kaleo* and means "to call." *Kaleo* can be understood as used in a classroom, when the teacher calls a student to the front of the class. The expression *church* has much the same meaning: its focus is also on people being called out, especially from among the nonbelieving. All who make up the church have been called.

Everyone is invited,[29] but not everyone answers Christ's call. For some, the voice of the Shepherd is drowned out by the cares of this life. They simply avoid the challenge of resisting sin[30] and exercising faith with all the other things Christians do that seem so laborious to them. Others fail to find fellowship with Jesus because they have fallen into the deception of false teaching.

## Religious Groups of Christ's Time

One looking into the history of religious sects at and around the time of Christ can draw parallels to the mindset of many Christians today. Two thousand years ago, there were several devout groups in Israel. The Pharisees and Sadducees were the largest denominations, and they were mentioned in the New Testament on several occasions. In the days Jesus walked the earth, most of Israel was keeping the Old Testament covenants. They observed the Sabbaths. They kept the feast days.

The nation of Israel was looking for a deliverer[31] as promised in the Scriptures; to free them from Roman rule. Four hundred years had passed since Israel had seen a prophet. Then the day came when John the Baptist began baptizing in the Jordan River. John had no phylacteries[32] upon his forehead nor did he look as spotless as the lawyers and scribes who came to see him. John's elegance was from within.

Israel's visible church had all the outward splendor of a sanctified group;[33] many were well dressed and freshly bathed, but some of the most distinguished ones were lacking what really counted—qualities such as "justice, mercy, and faithfulness."[34] When John saw "many of the Pharisees and Sadducees coming to where he was baptizing, he said to them: 'You brood of vipers'" (Matt. 3:7). These men were the highest-ranking leaders in Israel, but John weighed them on a scale of truth and found them lacking. These men attended the synagogue weekly and kept all of the required ordinances, and they were the most prominent of Israel's upper class. Yet John told them to repent of their wrongdoing and then be baptized; they refused. Instead of taking John's advice,[35] they publicly discredited him.

When Jesus spoke to them, he said, "Woe to you, teachers of the law and Pharisees, you hypocrites! You travel over land and sea to win a single convert, and when he becomes one, you make him twice as much a son of hell as you are" (Matt. 23:15). Christ claimed these Pharisees were ungodly men. He went on to say, "On the outside you appear to people as righteous but on the inside you are full of hypocrisy and wickedness" (Matt. 23:28).

If the scribes and Pharisees had been humble, God-seeking men, they might have repented and found righteousness.[36] The irony is that they were so devout in their outward practices, they mistakenly thought they were sanctified. They were missing the meaning of the Old Covenant laws; these teachers of Israel needed to do some learning themselves. All of their observances[37] were pointing to Christ, yet when they looked him in the face, they failed to recognize him. The scribes and Pharisees were members in Israel's visible church, but many weren't really a part of the true congregation. When Christ reproved them, explaining that genuine righteousness is from within, they quickly dismissed his words.

How many men and women today who are active in religion[38] wouldn't recognize Jesus if he showed up at their doors? How many people today would also quickly dismiss his words,[39] trusting beyond hope that mere ritual would save their souls? Among the visible church there are those who have failed the grace[40] of God. Instead of growing to maturity, they remain bound in religious ceremony.

## A Smaller Body within the Large Assembly

Even within the sanctified church, different people have different levels of commitment. I'm not speaking about salvation here: Christ's blood covers a multitude of sins—his grace is sufficient for us. Nevertheless, in the church at large, some are hot and others are lukewarm.

In the book of Revelation we find seven letters written to seven churches. Many scholars believe these churches represent church ages throughout history, with the seventh church representing the last church on earth. Let's read the letter to this church:

## The Church in Laodicea

> I know your deeds, that you are neither cold nor hot. I wish you were either one or the other! So, because you are lukewarm—neither hot nor cold—I am about to spit you out of my mouth. You

say, "I am rich; I have acquired wealth and do not need a thing." But you do not realize that you are wretched, pitiful, poor, blind and naked. I counsel you to buy from me gold refined in the fire, so you can become rich; and white clothes to wear, so you can cover your shameful nakedness; and salve to put on your eyes, so you can see. Those whom I love I rebuke and discipline. So be earnest, and repent. (Rev. 3:15–19)

## The Marriage Supper of the Lamb

On several occasions Jesus spoke of a heavenly marriage feast. He said, "Many will come from the east and the west, and will take their places at the feast with Abraham, Isaac and Jacob in the kingdom of heaven" (Matt. 8:11). Jesus alluded to this feast in parable after parable. He painted pictures of this event from many different perspectives. One man, after hearing of the marriage feast, said to Jesus, "Blessed is the man who will eat at the feast in the kingdom of God."[41] Jesus replied, saying: "A certain man was preparing a great banquet and invited many guests . . . ."[42] Christ went on to explain how the guests whom this man originally invited made excuses as to why they couldn't attend. So he had his servants go out in the streets and fill his house with anyone who would heed the call, including the poor, the crippled, and the blind. The lower-class people of the city gladly accepted the invitation, and ultimately the house was filled. Finally the man cried out, "Not one of those men who were [originally] invited will get a taste of my banquet."[43] This great feast is symbolic of an event that is on the horizon. The servants are gathering guests at this very hour. The Master's house will be filled.

## Outward Appearances

In this world by all outward appearances, many of us look unworthy to be invited to the Master's house; in the eyes of many religionists, we're the ones who are poor, crippled, and blind. Yet we're the ones who obey the Master's call. We're the ones who forsake the cares of this world and set out on a journey to spiritual perfection. Therefore the Master of the house (Jesus Christ) will reward us.

In another rendition of the great marriage feast, Christ adds more details:

> Then he said to his servants, "The wedding banquet is ready, but those I invited did not deserve to come. Go to the street corners and invite to the banquet anyone you find." So the servants went out into the streets and gathered all the people they could find, both good and bad, and the wedding hall was filled with guests. But when the king came in to see the guests, he noticed a man there who was not wearing wedding clothes. "Friend," he asked, "how did you get in here without wedding clothes?" The man was speechless. Then the king told the attendants, "Tie him hand and foot, and throw him outside, into the darkness, where there will be weeping and gnashing of teeth." For many are invited, but few are chosen. (Matt. 22:8–14)

Through the illustrations of a natural wedding banquet, Jesus is teaching us spiritual principles: The most obvious point Jesus expressed in his parables was that the cares of this life sidetracked many of the invited guests. This theme is presented many times. It's a stinging admonition and call to repentance for every man, woman, and child who unwittingly avoids God's invitation. The nation of Israel was implicated as the original invited guests; however, the sayings of Jesus are still relevant today. Now anyone with a callous heart who ignores the call of God may find himself or herself outside of Christ's fellowship.

"Jesus spoke to them again in parables, saying: 'The kingdom of heaven is like a king who prepared a wedding banquet for his son'" (Matt. 22:1–2). Surely the king in this parable represents God; the king's son represents Jesus Christ. Jesus also said: "When someone invites you to a wedding feast, do not take the place of honor, for a person more distinguished than you may have been invited. If so, the host who invited both of you will come and say to you, 'Give this man your seat.' Then, humiliated, you will have to take the least important place. But when you are invited, take the lowest place, so that when your host comes, he will say to you, 'Friend, move up to a better place.' Then you will be honored in the presence of all your fellow guests. For everyone who exalts himself will be humbled, and he who humbles himself will be exalted" (Luke 14:8–11).

Principles are being taught here. Christ wasn't all that worried about our precise etiquette during a wedding feast on earth. The guests' seating arrangement at the feast in his parable is an example of the coming kingdom. Jesus is teaching us eternal values, exhorting us to achieve our best standing in both this life and the life to come by humbling ourselves and becoming subservient to our peers.

## The Wedding Parable Is a Model

Envision a bride-to-be having a dream about her wedding day, yearning to be swept away from her ho-hum existence; suddenly a shining prince on a white horse sweeps her into his arms and takes her into a paradise land with crystal-clear waters and wondrous surroundings. She dreams on. In this wonderland they will live forever young with a depth of love that has no bounds. This bride's dream shadows the actual paradise waiting on the horizon for the ones Christ loves. A man and woman in wedded bliss are a natural model that has a supernatural counterpart.

From the very beginning, God's plan was to live in[44] and dwell[45] with his human children. God has longed to cherish his children. Through Christ, God will fulfill his plan. Jesus will ride up on a white horse[46] as a shining prince[47] and receive his bride[48] unto himself: "Blessed are those who are invited to the wedding supper of the Lamb!" (Rev. 19:9).

## Jesus Christ—a Greater Solomon

In the Song of Solomon, where it reads "My beautiful one, come with me," this is an illustration of the Rapture of the church. Solomon had many wives. The Scripture reads, "Sixty queens there may be, and eighty concubines, and virgins beyond number; but my dove, my perfect one is unique, the only daughter of her mother, the favorite of the one who bore her."[49] In the figurative language of the Song of Solomon, King Solomon represents Jesus Christ. The various classes of women in our text may represent the entire visible church; "the favorite of the one who bore her" is most likely a representation of a smaller number of people. In this illustration Solomon asks only one bride to come away with him, the *perfect one*—this designation may signify that this group of people has developed more spiritually than the general assembly.

Listen to what the general assembly cries out as Solomon takes his bride from among them: "Come back, come back, O Shulamite; come back, come back, that we may gaze upon you" (Song of Sol. 6:13).

## Will Jesus Catch Away a Halfhearted Church with Filthy Garments?

Some theologians are absolutely convinced that every man, woman, and child who has confessed Christ as Savior is guaranteed a position in the early Resurrection and Rapture. However, based on clear Scripture, this may not be the case. There are problems with this understanding, not only in the interpretation of our last text, but also in the less figurative words of Paul.

Jesus called Paul on the Damascus road as an apostle. Paul became an apostle of exceptional character. The Apostle Paul penned one-third of the New Testament under the inspiration of God. He dedicated his life to the furtherance of the Gospel. There's no doubt that Paul was a dedicated Christian; yet he was concerned about his own standing in Christ concerning the Rapture. He knew by revelation from the Holy Spirit that not every Christian would be found worthy of the first resurrection, and Paul, through the guiding of the Spirit, wrote out his concern for our enlightenment. His request to God is clearly stated. Paul is speaking: "I want to know Christ and the power of his resurrection and the fellowship of sharing in his sufferings, becoming like him in his death, and so, somehow, to attain to the resurrection from the dead" (Phil. 3:10–11). Sometimes the NIV does not bring out the full meaning of the original Greek language in which the New Testament was written. This is the case with our last passage. Two different words are used for the word "resurrection" in these verses. The word in verse 10 is *anastasis*, which literally means "a standing up again." This word is used for resurrection thirty-nine times in the New Testament. In verse 11, speaking about the resurrection Paul is striving for, the word *exanastasis* is used. This word is used only once in Scripture—in this verse; the emphasis is on *standing up* as well as *rising* or ascending.

Even though our modern Bible does not bring out the full meaning of the Greek, by using common sense we can circumvent the incomplete rendering of this text. For example, what resurrection could Paul be referring to? There are only two in Scripture. Is it possible Paul thought he might miss out on both? This is unlikely, seeing that apparently everyone who is not a part of the first resurrection will take part in the second. The most likely answer is that Paul was striving to be accounted worthy of the "first resurrection,"[50] which is the standing up and ascending of the faithful, which we call the Rapture.

## The Letter to the Laodiceans—Revisited

"I know your deeds, that you are neither cold nor hot. I wish you were either one or the other! So, because you are lukewarm—neither hot nor cold—I am about to spit you out of my mouth" (Rev. 3:15–16). What might this saying of Jesus symbolize? Quite frankly, the words "Arise, come, my darling; my beautiful one, come with me"[51] and "I am about to spit you out of my mouth" are opposed to each other. The most popular understanding of this last text is that this is a rebuke to the last church on earth.

Jesus is setting standards for his brothers and sisters to follow. Jesus is admonishing all those who have a shallow commitment to him to enter into a deeper relationship. There is no question Christ was addressing a church in this rebuke, for this Scripture is taken from a letter addressed to a church. Earlier in Revelation Jesus was seen standing among them[52] symbolically speaking.[53] The problem with this church is that these people are sure they are in need of nothing, yet they lack intimacy with Jesus. They are immature; they are not striving to walk worthy of the calling like the more mature ones because they thought they were toeing the line.

# Chapter 4

# SEALS AND HORSES

The word *apocalypse* is Greek for the English word "revelation." But what does the word *revelation* mean?

**rev·e·la·tion** (rĕ vé-la'shen) noun
1. a. The act of revealing or disclosing. b. Something revealed, especially a dramatic disclosure of something not previously known or realized.
2. *Theology.* A manifestation of divine will or truth.
3. **Revelation** (rĕvé-lā 'shen) *Abbr.* **Rev., Rv.** A book of the Bible.

Middle English *revelacion*, from Old French *revelation*, from Latin *revclātiô, revclātiôn-*, from *revclātus* past participle of *revclâre*, to reveal (Microsoft Encarta Reference Suite 99).

The act of disclosing, uncovering—making known something that is hidden—this is what *revelation* means; this uncovering of hidden prophecy is what the book of Revelation is all about. One looking into Revelation's pages should come away enlightened. Yet reading that book for most people only leaves them confused: why is that? Revelation is a picture book; it's like a movie fixed in time.

Many, after reading Revelation, come away from the experience with questions: Will the plagues be literal, with the oceans turning to blood and the sun scorching men with great heat, or could these illustrations be figurative, having a different meaning entirely? Surely literal fire[54] will not be coming out of the mouths of the two witnesses.[55]

Bible prophecy is always easier to understand when looking back on it rather than forward to it. In this and the following chapters, I will offer possible models of Revelation's plagues, explaining what we might expect to see.

## Seven Seals

As Jesus begins breaking open each of Revelation's seven wax seals, a series of events come to pass. The first four seals send four horsemen riding through the earth, bringing in famine and death and quickly establishing Antichrist's regime. The fifth seal sets up the killing machine Antichrist will use upon Christians. The sixth seal denotes great apostasy from the faith. The seventh seal contains seven trumpets—following is a series of seven trumpet blasts. This is symbolic of heaven's battle and intended victory,[56] each blast having an impact on earth. The last three trumpet blasts are called *woes*. The seventh trumpet, or final woe, contains the bowl[57] judgments. As the final bowl is poured out, Armageddon[58] takes place.

In the first place, we might ask why should something Jesus is doing in heaven initiate a demonic uprising on earth? Christ is shown opening Revelation's mortgage scroll (the deed to the earth). He is about to reclaim the domain Adam forfeited to Satan. Jesus is redeeming the earth with all the souls that have faith in his atonement. As the new owner, Christ is opening the deed to make sure everything is in order. But everything is not in order! The whole earth is filled with wickedness, and this shall not stand. Satan, realizing that time is short, musters all of his forces into action and quickly brings about his final conquest. However, as Jesus loosens the last wax seal of the scroll, Satan is no longer triumphant over mankind. In a last-ditch effort to thwart Christ's victory, Satan brings the world to the brink of destruction during the battle of Armageddon—at which time Christ returns to the Mount of Olives and saves the world.

## Four Horses Bringing In a Brave New World

What does a horse symbolize? Strength! Battle! The ability to cover large distances! What do horsemen do? They ride. Revelation's horses have been waiting at the starting gate for a very long time. When they and their riders journey through the earth, they will take the world by storm. These horsemen are illustrations of fallen spirits who have been granted power before the courts of God to influence men and bring pestilence and death upon earth. The deception these angels manifest may also be a sign to the Middle Eastern people that their deliverer/messiah is at hand. "The coming of the lawless one will be in accordance with the work of Satan displayed in all kinds of counterfeit miracles, signs and wonders, and in every sort of evil that deceives those who are perishing" (2 Thess. 2:9–10).

## Seal One—the First Horse Rides

> I watched as the Lamb opened the first of the seven seals. Then I heard one of the four living creatures say in a voice like thunder, "Come!" I looked, and there before me was a white horse! Its rider held a bow, and he was given a crown, and he rode out as a conqueror bent on conquest. (Rev. 6:1–2)

A white horse: what better color could have been used to depict a conqueror? When this first seal is broken, John hears a clap of thunder; could this signify a sudden conquest? The words "and he was given a crown" are noteworthy, for Satan has a crown to give. He has dominion over "all the kingdoms of the world."[59] In the Gospel of Luke, Satan tempted Christ with his authority to rule the planet. He said to Jesus, "I will give you all their authority and splendor, for it has been given to me, and I can give it to anyone I want to" (Luke 4:6).

The rider of the white horse "held a bow." This symbolism denotes weaponry and battle. The text itself states that this horseman "rode out as a conqueror bent on conquest." This depicts nations being overthrown during the time this horse rides. The Scriptures mention "the spirit of the Antichrist, which you have heard is coming,"[60] which is a reference to demonic activity. We have fallen angels in the world today; they are already at work influencing men. There are also angels so wicked that God has them bound until the righteous are sealed; then those spirits will be let loose to torment mankind.

## Seal Two—the Second Horse Rides

> When the Lamb opened the second seal, I heard the second living creature say, "Come!" Then another horse came out, a fiery red one. Its rider was given power to take peace from the earth and to make men slay each other. To him was given a large sword. (Rev. 6:3–4)

The color red was given to this horse to depict blood! The large sword this horseman receives is a symbolic illustration of the massive force the rider will manifest upon earth. What does a sword do? It kills! Men wield weapons of death upon this earth; the rider of the red horse has been given power to influence mankind to kill one another, possibly bringing the earth into a state of crisis, setting the stage for Antichrist's entrance. The man of sin will probably come upon the world scene hiding under a false cloak as a man of peace, a savior—an influential world leader who could very well unite the Islamic and Jewish people for a season.

## A Tangent with Judas in It

Fallen angels—that is, demons—can plant thoughts in people's minds; they can play on people's emotions. Demons accomplish their goals by manipulating their unsuspecting hosts like a puppeteer pulling on strings. Demons work more easily through men and women who are unaware of their existence, especially the unbelieving—men in sync with the forces of evil do their bidding. This could be how Satan initially takes peace from the earth. Many people are pawns in Satan's hand, fulfilling his goals while condemning their own souls.

Back when Jesus walked the earth, Satan entered Judas and worked in him, plotting to have Jesus killed. What reward did Judas receive for his appointment as Satan's right-hand man? "With the reward he got for his wickedness, Judas bought a field; there he fell headlong, his body burst open and all his intestines spilled out" (Acts 1:18). Judas was driven to such torment after he betrayed Jesus that he ended his own life by hanging himself. That was just the beginning of sorrows for Judas, for the Scriptures express: "Woe to that man who betrays the Son of Man! It would be better for him if he had not been born" (Matt. 26:24).

This miserable, hell-bound Judas was not aware that the devil had entered him and played on his emotions. Judas was doing the devil's bidding for so long he had taken on Satan's image. Judas was stealing money from Jesus and lying right to his face. Judas should have known the Lord was aware of his evil schemes, but his heart was hardened; he had forsaken the truth and went about fulfilling his own lusts. In his twisted mind, Judas probably thought he could get away with Christ's betrayal; however, as Satan was lying in wait to ensnare Jesus through him, it was Judas' soul he was also entrapping.

Judas justified his actions by believing the temporary reward of money was well worth any potential judgment he might face. Apparently he convinced himself that either God would overlook his transgression or, at the very least, the judgment would not be so bad. Judas' life is a good representation of men and women who serve Satan today. Peace will be taken from the earth by the manipulation of wicked men through powerful angels bent on doing Satan's bidding.

## The Powers of This Dark World

In the book of Ephesians, Satan and his demon forces are called "the powers of this dark world" (Eph. 6:12) Darkness demands that Satan's subjects have no light. The devil's followers have no truth to guide them in their resolve. As the devil restrains the light of truth from his followers, there is no threat of them seeing what a detrimental position they are holding. They are blind to the truth that the evil one is lord in their hearts.

What wise person walking in the light of God's understanding would ever choose Satan as lord? If all the evidence were laid out in plain view, that one would run from the hideous beast he was in league with to the loving arms of the heavenly Father. That's why the devil surrounds his subjects in darkness. Satan blinds their minds, as it is written, "The god of this age has blinded the minds of unbelievers, so that they cannot see the light of the gospel" (2 Cor. 4:4). The devil reigns through deception.

When the four horsemen ride through the earth bringing about changes in the attitudes of mankind, they will accomplish their goals quickly. Many will be unaware that evil forces are at work in them.

## Seal Three—the Third Horse Rides

> When the Lamb opened the third seal, I heard the third living creature say, "Come!" I looked, and there before me was a black horse! Its rider was holding a pair of scales in his hand. Then I heard what sounded like a voice among the four living creatures, saying, "A quart of wheat for a day's wages, and three quarts of barley for a day's wages, and do not damage the oil and the wine." (Rev. 6:5–6)

Black represents spiritual darkness. Balances represent judgment. If we put a day's pay on one side of the balance scale this horseman is holding and look at the other side of the scale, this verse shows that one would get little food in return. This third horseman brings pestilence and famine into the land.

To understand what these horsemen are, we should keep in mind that "power was given unto" them. Remember how Satan pleaded before the courts of God to smite Job and his house and was given power to do so? The devil and his angels received power to cause fire to come down from heaven and destroy Job's sheep and also those tending them. The devil also influenced the Sabeans and the Chaldeans to rob Job's livestock and kill Job's servants. Satan even had the power to cause a violent wind to destroy Job's eldest son's house, killing all those inside.

At the very time Jesus is opening the seals on the mortgage scroll to inspect the claim, Satan will be lashing out with great force. This planet could suffer massive environmental disasters as a result of these horses. It's possible we could see holy wars in which men could become crazed enough to pollute their enemies' cities or water supplies with nuclear or biochemical contamination.

## Seal Four—the Fourth Horse Rides

> When the Lamb opened the fourth seal, I heard the voice of the fourth living creature say, "Come!" I looked, and there before me was a pale horse! Its rider was named Death, and Hades was following close behind him. They were given power over a fourth of the earth to kill by sword, famine and plague, and by the wild beasts of the earth. (Rev. 6:7–8)

This spotted, pale gray horse is symbolic of a lingering death. "The wild beasts of the earth" may represent the Antichrist's religious and political systems these horsemen establish. The government under Antichrist will kill with hunger: anyone who refuses to take the Antichrist's mark will not be allowed to buy food. This Antichrist system will also kill with death—which means eternal separation from God. It's a sick spiritual state brought about through deception and sin. Surely observing Antichrist's religious ideology and receiving his mark will bring mankind into spiritual death.

> A third angel followed them and said in a loud voice: "If anyone worships the beast and his image and receives his mark on the forehead or on the hand, he, too, will drink of the wine of God's fury, which has been poured full strength into the cup of his wrath. He will be tormented with burning sulfur in the presence of the holy angels and of the Lamb. And the smoke of their torment rises for ever and ever. There is no rest day or night for those who worship the beast and his image, or for anyone who receives the mark of his name." (Rev. 14:9–11)

Some horses go into the north country,[61] which represents Russia. Their influence in Russia will have worked, for Russia is one of the nations mentioned in Ezekiel that come against Jerusalem in the battle of Armageddon. Christian nations, at the time the four horses ride through the earth, will not suffer the effects of these plagues nearly as much as certain Middle Eastern countries, such as Turkey, Iran, Ethiopia, and Libya, because the work of the wicked angels will be hindered by God's people. The promises of divine blessing and the forewarnings of divine cursing as spelled out in Scripture will still be in effect when the horses ride.

## The Four Horses of Zechariah

The four horses from Zechariah and the four horses of the Apocalypse are different views of the same horses. The dappled horse of Zechariah is the pale horse in Revelation.

> The first chariot had red horses, the second black, the third white, and the fourth dappled—all of them powerful. I asked the angel who was speaking to me, "What are these, my lord?" The angel answered me, "These are the four spirits of heaven, going out from standing in the presence of the Lord of the whole world. The one with the black horses is going toward the north country, the one with the white horses toward the west, and the one with the dappled horses toward the south." When the powerful horses went out, they were straining to go throughout the earth. And he said, "Go throughout the earth!" So they went throughout the earth. (Zech. 6:2–7)

We see in the book of Job that "One day the angels came to present themselves before the Lord, and Satan also came with them. The Lord said to Satan, 'Where have you come from?' Satan answered the Lord, 'From roaming through the earth and going back and forth in it'" (Job 1:6–7b). Evil spirits roam this earth. There are definite parallels between satanic activity and these horses in Zechariah and Revelation.

## Mountains—and the Woman Who Sits upon Them

"I looked up again—and there before me were four chariots coming out from between two mountains—mountains of bronze!" (Zech. 6:1). Mountains in Bible prophecy are illustrations depicting world empires. "This calls for a mind with wisdom. The seven heads are seven hills on which the woman sits" (Rev. 17:9). These seven mountains represent the seven world empires this earth has had since the beginning of creation: Egypt, Assyria, Babylon, Media-Persia, Greece, Rome, and the Antichrist's world government to come. In prophetic history, these chariots and horses will appear between the close of this present dispensation and the beginning of Antichrist's dominion.

A woman in Bible prophecy is always a church. In the case of the woman who sits upon the seven hills, it's an illustration of a false religious system. False religion will be a major component of the new world order. Speaking of this subject, John recorded: "I saw that the woman was drunk with the blood of the saints, the blood of those who bore testimony to Jesus" (Rev. 17:6). In the New World Order, killing the Christians will be considered a holy cleansing.

## The Fifth Seal—Martyrs

> When he opened the fifth seal, I saw under the altar the souls of those who had been slain because of the word of God and the testimony they had maintained. They called out in a loud voice, "How long, Sovereign Lord, holy and true, until you judge the inhabitants of the earth and avenge our blood?"

> Then each of them was given a white robe, and they were told to wait a little longer, until the number of their fellow servants and brothers who were to be killed as they had been was completed. (Rev. 6:9–11)

In this last verse, martyrs throughout history are told to wait a little longer for God's judgment to be administered upon earth because there are still more martyrs to come. When Antichrist sets up his killing machine to eliminate all who will not take his mark, it's possible we will see martyrdom on a major scale. This will be the true test for halfhearted, partially committed men and women who profess Jesus as Savior. It's inevitable that multitudes will fall from the faith, submitting to the edicts of the man of sin, rather than suffer death.

## The Sixth Seal—Apostasy

> I watched as he opened the sixth seal. There was a great earthquake. The sun turned black like sackcloth made of goat hair, the whole moon turned blood red, and the stars in the sky fell to earth, as late figs drop from a fig tree when shaken by a strong wind. The sky receded like a scroll, rolling up, and every mountain and island was removed from its place. (Rev. 6:12–14)

It's interesting to note the figurative language in verse 14: "The sky receded like a scroll, rolling up." Seeing that the deed to the earth is also a scroll as recorded in the same book, it would seem that an illustration of a scroll rolling up might point to a change in the deed's status. Surely the illustration "every mountain and island was removed from its place" is speaking of a change in dispensations.

Let's look at verse 13 of this last passage again, focusing on the stars: "And the stars in the sky fell to earth, as late figs drop from a fig tree when shaken by a strong wind." Here is a good example of the symbolism in Revelation and how to understand it. First, let's ignore that Revelation was written in symbols. We will assume the stars in this verse are natural and see where this understanding takes us. If we agree that the sun is a typical star and there are millions of stars in our galaxy alone, then we take into account that the diameter of even one medium-size star is over one hundred times that of Earth. Then add to this the account recorded in the next four verses of this same chapter: after the stars fall to the earth, men are complaining about the great day of the Lamb's wrath. This leaves us with a serious problem. If the stars that fall to the earth are natural, how could Antichrist compile an army for that great battle of Armageddon? No one would be complaining because everyone would be dead. Nevertheless, stars do fall to the earth. This verse is speaking of apostasy.

What do stars falling have to do with a fig tree being shaken, symbolically speaking? The nation of Israel is described as a fig tree and also an olive tree in the Bible. Men are likened unto trees. Jesus cursed a fig tree because there was no fruit on it. Yet it was the right time of the season for fruit, and there were even leaves on the tree, which Christ saw from a distance, showing that fruit should have been there. Men produce fruit out of a good heart. The hearts of the men of Israel were unfruitful, so God cut down the tree.

John the Baptist said, "The ax is already at the root of the trees."[62] John warned Israel to bring forth fruit. However, John's words were not heeded and John was beheaded. There's no question John was a prophet sent from God. However, the wind of adversity shook at those Pharisees, and because they loved not the truth, they were cast to the earth symbolically and lost their position in heaven.

Yet the book of Revelation is written about the future, not what Israel did in the past! While the symbolism remains true, the time frame is wrong. The nation of Israel rejected the Messiah, and they were cut off just like John warned. A new branch was grafted into the tree. In the book of Romans we see that the Gentiles are the new branch.

The stars that fall in Revelation are weak-minded Christians who have a poor foundation, and in their day of adversity, when they are shaken, they are cast to the earth, symbolically. The symbolism of stars falling in Rev. 6:13 depicts a great falling away of Christians from the faith due to persecution from the Antichrist government.

## Figurative Interpretation Continues

We know there will be a great falling away from the Christian faith when the Antichrist imposes his will upon mankind. Could the understanding of this prophecy have something to do with this apostasy? Things like the moon turning to blood and the sun turning black can have figurative meanings. The moon may represent the old covenant with all of the laws and ordinances. It has no light of its own, yet it was given to us as a light. Only when we have the light of the sun cast upon the moon do we see it shine forth. All of the Old Testament ceremonial ordinances can be understood in the light of Christ. He is the sun[63] in Bible prophecy.

Blood may point to his blood atonement. The sun turning to darkness may represent a lack of spiritual enlightenment. When the great apostasy from the Christian faith befalls mankind, spiritual darkness[64] will cover the land. Even though the covenant[65] is dripping with the blood of Christ's atonement, people will no longer enter in because light is no longer being cast. The earth has chosen darkness, so darkness it was given. Even the stars withdrew their light.

## A Poor Understanding

Many Bible teachers and authors have a poor understanding of Revelation's imagery. These men and women simply haven't done their homework researching the Scriptures. If these instructors would go back to their studies and pore over the mountains of Old Testament illustrations and parallel texts, then they would see the Old Testament counterparts paint a far different picture of the days to come than what they teach. Instead of offering opinions based on popular ideology, these people could bring forth a more realistic view of the coming plagues.

## Deception Is on the Horizon

The reason some of us will be deceived in the days ahead is partly because Revelation's eschatology will unfold in a drastically different manner than what we expect. Consider this: Satan has always worked in subtle ways; getting mankind to doubt his existence is one of his greatest achievements. If he were to let the wicked know he was real, they might put two and two together and realize that Jesus Christ and the judgment day must also be real. The devil will not surrender his best strategy so easily—he will continue to hide his existence even as he torments his victims. Deception is coming on a major scale: Revelation's pages foretell a time of gross spiritual darkness.

For thousands of years, Satan and his entourage have been blinding the minds of the unenlightened and simultaneously pulling on their emotions in an effort to accomplish their goals. As the horsemen ride throughout the earth, they don't have the power to kill men directly. They stir up the minds of their victims and let them go rampaging. Even during the time of trumpets, when demonic activity will reach its peak, much of the world won't realize they are standing at the crossroads of annihilation. The light of the gospel was ignored in the day when laborers were working hard, bringing in the harvest; now the night is come when no man can work.

Chapter  5

# THE MIDNIGHT HOUR

Mankind has entered a new age—a brave new world. Lawlessness abounds. The love of many has grown cold. A battle is raging, yet most are unaware of the underlying forces pushing forward, sweeping through the earth, working to dominate the planet and set up Satan's prince as king.[66]

Now the battle is in the hearts of men, but when the man of lawlessness arrives, we will see the war; the killing fields will be our streets. This man will come upon the scene with great deception. The whole world will marvel over him. He will establish a one-world order. Many, unaware of the true nature of the beast, will welcome him as God. "At last," they will say, "the messiah from the seed of David is here to rule and bring in the millennium." Some will think the kingdom of heaven has come to earth, for it is written in the Scriptures that God will rule his people through Christ in the coming millennium. But this is the false christ that Jesus said men would receive.

Before the devil is bound,[67] he will be allowed one last hurrah. Man is not headed for a golden age. What lies ahead for mankind is gross spiritual darkness;[68] this will be an age where wickedness abounds. The father of lies[69] is about to herald his greatest lie. Antichrist will have a sales pitch so refined that people will receive his twisted illusions with itching ears.[70] As the clock ticks down, one thing is certain: a new world order will arrive with man united in a common cause under the mastery of Satan.

As this planet spins ever closer to the time of Antichrist, earth will reel from the absence of light; man will strive against the Spirit of God. Because mankind has abandoned God's ways and pursued wickedness, Satan will be granted his appointed season to commence the ancient plan.

## Antichrists of Ancient Time

The history of Rome gives us a picture of events that parallel the midnight hour. Antichrist had counterparts throughout history. In the days Christ walked this earth, Rome was a world government with the Emperor Augustus as its world leader. Augustus was chief priest over the pagan cults. He held the title of *pontifex maximus*.[71] Legend has it that a god in the guise of a serpent visited Augustus' mother in the temple of Apollo nine months before his birth.[72]

The intelligence ruling Rome was a dark force. Satan maintained the real authority. It was Satan who stood behind the office Augustus held. The emperor was merely his front man. Augustus' program of building new pagan temples and restoring the old religion was Satan's scheme to thwart the worship of the true God. The laws instituted to promote pagan worship were supposedly issued for the sake of humanity. People were persuaded to worship false gods for the good of mankind. It was taught that the powerful gods of nature (Janus, Jupiter, Juno, Mars, and Vesta) had to be appeased to keep calamities such as earthquakes, drought, and famine from afflicting the people.

As time passed, ancient Rome's laws concerning the worship of these gods were rigidly enforced. Even the deified Caesars needed to be worshipped. If any man refused to reverence the gods, he was allegedly putting the whole empire in jeopardy, for it was thought that well-pleased gods protected Rome. Emperors in Rome, as time went by, became more powerful. They also became immoral.

## Gods and Monsters

Merely for his own pleasure, Caius Caligula often had innocent people tortured while he was entertaining. Caligula was the first Roman emperor who insisted on being a god in his lifetime. Emperors before him had been pronounced gods after death, but Caligula had statues of himself placed in Jewish synagogues,[73] and since he considered himself a god, he demanded that the Jews worship his image. His image would also have been placed in the Jerusalem temple if he hadn't been assassinated before that order could be carried out.

## The Problem with Christians

Domitian, the younger brother of Titus, was elected emperor in the year A.D. 81. He demanded that his officers and staff call him *dominus et dues*, which in English translates as "Lord and God."[74] These mortal men were gods in their own minds. They would not tolerate other gods standing in a place of eminence before them. Christians were a real problem because their faith rested upon Scripture. They understood that "there is but one God, the Father."[75] They refused to worship the false gods of Rome. Christians at that time in history were a threat to the solidarity of the Roman Empire. It was getting to the point where the only acceptable solution was to completely abolish Christianity. Emperor Domitian arrested some Christians who would not revere his divinity. They were condemned to death and subsequently executed. It's rather ironic that the charge of atheism was hung upon these faithful believers.

In A.D. 250 under Emperor Decius, a new law was drafted: all those who offended the gods would be arrested. But if the accused Christians would publicly pay homage to Rome's gods by pouring out wine before them and renouncing their Christianity,[76] then all charges would be dropped and they would be set free. Decius issued an edict ordering everyone to perform public acts of worship. Anyone refusing was put to death. Certificates of conformity were issued to the superintendent of sacrifices at the time of sacrifice. This registration avowed worship in the state-approved cults.

## At the Midnight Hour

History will repeat itself. To see how the devil will rule the world at the midnight hour, let's consider how he ruled the world in the past. Satan was behind the Roman edict that ensured the worship of false gods and prohibited Christianity. It was the devil who put it in the heart of the emperor to kill all Christians in the name of humanity.

In the new world order under the Emperor Antichrist, everyone will need a mark of conformity to demonstrate that they have registered. This registration will be granted after they perform the required worship. "All inhabitants of the earth will worship the beast" (Rev. 13:8). Just as it was in ancient Rome, so will it be again: Christians who will not worship Satan's emperor will become fugitives from justice.

## The Birth of the Harlot Church

As time went on in ancient Rome, it became evident that Christianity was not going away. It appeared that killing the Christians only made the gospel more influential.

The preaching of the cross was bringing men to salvation; therefore Satan was determined to change the teaching. He developed another scheme to thwart Christ's victory. Salvation, as a gift that could not be earned,[77] would soon be changed to a rite for those who followed church precepts with all the ordinances[78] that were set in place by the governing "father." The devil set out to cloud the pure water of the Word with the bitter herbs of false doctrine.

When Constantine and his army invaded Rome, killing the old emperor, he found his new empire in a state of conflict. Rome was torn apart because of Christian persecution. In an effort to stabilize Rome, Constantine issued the Edict of Milan,[79] which made Christianity legal.

Emperor Constantine was raised in the upper class of society. Intellectuals from the schools of higher learning where Constantine was educated regarded Christianity as a crude[80] religion in language, status, and outward appearance. It had none of the ceremonial festivities practiced by the pagans. Constantine made Christianity fashionable[81] to the higher classes. He took the title of *pontifex maximus*,[82] standing as chief priest over the pagan cults. He then brought the pagan priests into the church, giving them high administrative offices. The church was singing a new song. Everyone was invited, yes, compelled to join.

Anytime a controversy arose concerning what doctrines to teach the people, an appointed council of bishops would define and draft a creed to which all parties could agree. Doctrinal debates that earlier would have run their course among theologians now became political issues. The worship services of the Roman church became filled with mysticism. Instead of wine representing Christ's blood, the priest would conjure up real blood from wine through an elaborate ceremony. This ritual as practiced by the Catholic Church today is called transubstantiation.[83]

The Roman church became a well-oiled religious mechanism. Pope Innocent III[84] claimed to be "Vicar of Christ and God." He brought "the papacy to the zenith of its power."[85]

Antichrist will have religion too. This religious system is described as a harlot in the book of Revelation: "MYSTERY BABYLON THE GREAT, THE MOTHER OF PROSTITUTES AND OF THE ABOMINATIONS OF THE EARTH" (Rev. 17:5). This "prostitute religion," as prophesied in Scripture and instituted through Satan, had a partial fulfillment in the Roman Catholic Church;[86] its final fulfillment will be with the order Antichrist and the false prophet will endorse. With the devil running the show, he will certainly be spitting out his own twisted views[87] on spiritual matters. His authority will be far worse for mankind than any of his predecessors.[88]

## The Image of the Beast

Like the popes of ancient times, this new ruler will claim to be "the Vicar of God." Standing as God on earth, this one will demand worship. "Men worshiped the dragon because he had given authority to the beast" (Rev. 13:4a). While the man of lawlessness himself may be considered "the image of the beast" (Rev. 13:15), many believe this may also refer to a vast telecommunications system.

## The Mark of the Beast

In the new world order under Antichrist, a campaign to wipe Christians from off the face of the earth will be initiated. He shall issue an edict forcing "everyone small and great, rich and poor, free and slave, to receive a mark on his right hand or on his forehead, so that no one could buy or sell unless he had the mark" (Rev. 13:16–17). This decree will be issued as the new king attempts to accomplish the prime directive: dominion over mankind. The false prophet will endorse the Antichrist's commission through the miracles[89] he performs, endorsing the decree causing "all[90] who refused to worship the image to be killed."[91]

Using modern technology, Antichrist will keep those who will not reverence him from any kind of money exchange. This will most likely be done through computer networks and a cashless society. A mark that can be read with a scanner will be utilized in Antichrist's government. Without the mark, it will be impossible to function in the new age. Several logical reasons will be given to establish this system. The government will have a running account of all monetary transactions. With the mark on each person, credit card theft and false identification will be impossible. Cash with all its problems—like robbery—will be a thing of the past.

Can you imagine a middle-aged man, with two cars, a house half paid for, and a family, coming home from work and telling his wife and two young daughters that from now on they will be driven from their home to live as fugitives, all because he will not submit to the veneration of the new world leader and accept the mark?

This may seem like too high a price to pay in order to stay within God's good graces. However, the people who endorse the Antichrist's policies and worship his image will, in fact, be worshipping the devil and contributing to his rebellion.

## Christianity Will Be Abolished

Jesus said, "A time is coming when anyone who kills you will think he is offering a service to God."[92] In the people's minds, the execution of Christians will be necessary. The Christian religion will be blamed for much of the world's problems. It will be taught that by uniting mankind through Antichrist's administration, we will find stability.

However, Christians will understand that receiving this mark and worshiping the beast will void the grace they possessed in Christ. This message shall be proclaimed throughout the earth: "If anyone worships the beast and his image and receives his mark on the forehead or on the hand, he, too, will drink of the wine of God's fury, which has been poured full strength into the cup of his wrath. He will be tormented with burning sulfur in the presence of the holy angels and of the Lamb" (Rev. 14:9–10).

Christians are given assurance from Scripture that "God will wipe away every tear from their eyes."[93] These strong-willed saints will be rewarded for their faith, as it is written: "Blessed are the dead who die in the Lord from now on. 'Yes,' says the Spirit, 'they will rest from their labor, for their deeds will follow them." (Rev. 14:13). When Satan, through his religious order, is pushing hard

## Israel Is Still Looking for Christ

Almost two thousand years have passed since Jesus walked this earth. Jesus fit the messianic prophecies. An unbiased individual reading the Bible and seeking truth would come to the conclusion that Jesus was the true Christ.

God had warned[94] Israel to accept the coming prophet. However, when Christ's gospel hindered the influence of Israel's religious leaders, those wicked men plotted to kill him, saying he had violated one of their holy laws. The truth is, they hated[95] Jesus without reason.

These unscrupulous religious men paid Judas to betray Jesus into the soldiers' hands and then, through lies and deception, brought Jesus before the Roman judicial system. There they paraded one false witness after another before Pontius Pilate, who stood as governor and had the authority as judge to condemn men to death. However, Pilate's heart was purer than that group of austere men who were determined to have Jesus killed. He struggled to set Christ free. When the crowd would not allow that, he then washed his hands before the people and declared he was innocent of Christ's blood.

Pilate then turned his fate over to the pleadings of the crowd. When the people cried out, "Let his blood be on us and on our children,"[96] Pilate allowed his soldiers to bring Jesus to the common hall. From there, they took Christ to Golgotha and crucified him to the mocking cries of the religious leaders. The "king of the Jews"[97] was never ordained. Israel had their delivering king crucified.

Many claim the Messiah of Scripture was supposed to usher in the kingdom of God. Because Jesus died without fulfilling this commission, they say he was not the genuine Messiah. Therefore, the nation of Israel and many Jewish people worldwide are still looking for Messiah to come and rule as king, proclaiming Israel his faithful people and setting up the kingdom of God in Jerusalem.

Jesus prophesied: "I have come in my Father's name, and you do not accept me; but if someone else comes in his own name, you will accept him."[98] Two thousand years later at the midnight hour, a false christ will appear and alongside him a false prophet. The nation of Israel will accept them with open arms. Together, they will bring in a new age in which once more a single king will rule the world.

# Chapter 6

# TRUMPETS—SOUNDING OF JUDGMENT

## Revelation's Scroll with Seven Seals

Back in the time when Revelation was penned, there were no printing presses. Documents were handwritten on papyrus and rolled up as scrolls. Revelation's scroll represents a mortgage agreement. It was the custom in that period to seal the scroll of the mortgaged property so that no one could tamper with the deed. Another scroll would accompany the sealed scroll, and people would refer to it concerning the contents of the sealed scroll. The sealed scroll would be opened only at the time the property was transferred. The new owner would then inspect the real deed and make sure everything was in order.

The scroll in Revelation 5 represents the deed to the earth. Whoever holds it has the right to rule. When the last seal is loosed and the scroll is opened, the new owner will take possession of his property. God is shown symbolically sitting on the throne; He has possession of the scroll. Jesus is found worthy[99] to take the scroll from the Father's hand and open it. Jesus is redeeming the earth along with all the souls of men found worthy of redemption. He is receiving the right to rule the world at the very moment Antichrist's world government is in full power. There will be a war in heaven at that time, and Satan will be expelled. The Prince of Life, whom God ordained—Jesus, the one whom all of creation will proclaim to be worthy of the throne—will dethrone the devil and set up a new government in righteousness.

> Then I saw in the right hand of him who sat on the throne a scroll with writing on both sides and sealed with seven seals. And I saw a mighty angel proclaiming in a loud voice, "Who is worthy to break the seals and open the scroll?" But no one in heaven or on earth or under the earth could open the scroll or even look inside it. I wept and wept because no one was found who was worthy to open the scroll or look inside. Then one of the elders said to me, "Do not weep! See, the Lion of the tribe of Juda, the Root of David, has triumphed. He is able to open the scroll and its seven seals." (Rev. 5:1-5)

John was told that a mighty lion with stellar ancestry had triumphed! So John probably expected to see some powerful figure take hold of the scroll. This would not be the case. What John saw next was a lamb looking as if it had been slain, clutching an antique scroll as old as the earth itself, with ancient writings upon it within and without, and seven wax seals holding it closed. This feeble lamb tore open the final seal.

Why would the powerful Lion of Judah now have the appearance of a slain sacrificial lamb? Because God has taken the frail things of this world and made them strong; through death, that lamb became more powerful than any lion. Jesus, taking on the role of a sacrificial lamb, "purchased men." "When he opened the seventh seal, there was silence in heaven for about half an hour. And I saw the seven angels who stand before God, and to them were given seven trumpets" (Rev. 8:1-2).

# Trumpets—Sounding of Judgment

## A Trumpet Is a Shophar

> Blow the trumpet in Zion; sound the alarm on my holy hill. Let all who live in the land tremble, for the day of the LORD is coming. It is close at hand. (Joel 2:1)

The Hebrew trumpet in this passage is called a shophar; it was traditionally made from a ram's horn and was used in ancient Israel during war as a rallying cry. As the final seal of Revelation's mortgage scroll is broken, seven of these trumpets are given to seven angels. These trumpet judgments have significant meaning. They also have a definite purpose—to drive Antichrist from the throne.

Understanding that Revelation was written in symbols, let's look to Scripture for a physical example of trumpets being blown and then put together a model of what the trumpets in our study might signify. In the Old Testament book of Joshua, there's a written record of Israel's conquest of Jericho; the Lord spoke to Joshua telling him to lay siege on that city, saying, "Have seven priests carry trumpets of rams' horns in front of the ark. On the seventh day, march around the city seven times, with the priests blowing the trumpets. When you hear them sound a long blast on the trumpets, have all the people give a loud shout; then the wall of the city will collapse" (Josh. 6:4–6). The long trumpet blast according to Jewish tradition is called "the last trump."

The Israelites did as the Lord commanded and the wall of Jericho fell. No earthly weapon was used to bring down that wall; the battle was won through a work in the Spirit. The Lord promised Israel the city if Israel fought the battle according to His statutes. Israel did just as the Lord commanded, and He was faithful in giving them the victory. In the last days, Christians will be facing impenetrable walls also; yet it is recorded that once more God's people will be faithful. Then as Revelation's final trumpet begins to sound, the victory[100] will be ours.

## The Chronology of the Apocalypse

These trumpet judgments spell the end of Antichrist's regime, with the seventh trumpet containing Revelation's seven bowls of wrath. We can be fairly certain that much of the three and a half[101] years that the Antichrist was given to rule earth has passed before this time of trumpets begins. In Revelation, events escalate on a successive scale: to build a working model of Revelation's time frame, let's make some reasonable assumptions. Let's consider that the same amount of time will expire between the loosing of all seven of the scroll's wax seals. Let's also consider a seven-year time frame with each seal lasting one year. If this is the case, the breakdown of the main events in Revelation could follow this pattern: the first six seals take up six years, which is six-sevenths of Revelation's total time frame. This means the trumpet judgments, which are contained in the seventh seal, would occur during the seventh and final year. Within the seventh trumpet plague, there are seven bowls of wrath; therefore, all seven bowls will have the same duration as one of the trumpet plagues, meaning the seven bowls will last approximately seven weeks. Apparently, as we get closer to Armageddon, the judgments will follow each other in rapid succession, with each plague being more severe than the preceding plague.

How long did the rain fall in Noah's day—forty days? However, please keep in mind that Noah went into that ark one week before the rain fell. The ark of Noah is a model of the Rapture of the Church. Even as it was in Noah's day, God's faithful who ascend, riding the ark of God's provision, will be taken from this planet in the days before his wrath is poured out. If our working model is correct, we will ride, returning with the Captain of our salvation, Jesus Christ, seven weeks later, just like the former Captain Noah and the faithful ones did in their generation.

In Noah's day, everything was going along somewhat normally until Noah entered into the ark.[102] If the earth had shown powerful indications of a coming storm, the people should have taken heed to Noah's message.

## The Day and Hour Unknown

> No one knows about that day or hour, not even the angels in heaven, nor the Son, but only the Father. Be on guard! Be alert! You do not know when that time will come. It's like a man going away: He leaves his house and puts his servants in charge, each with his assigned task, and tells the one at the door to keep watch. Therefore keep watch because you do not know when the owner of the house will come back—whether in the evening, or at midnight, or when the rooster crows, or at dawn. If he comes suddenly, do not let him find you sleeping. What I say to you, I say to everyone: "Watch!" (Mark 13:32–36)

## Protection from the Trumpet Plagues

John records that before any trumpet sounds, the servants of God are sealed. "After this I saw four angels standing at the four corners of the earth, holding back the four winds of the earth to prevent any wind from blowing on the land or on the sea or on any tree. Then I saw another angel coming up from the east, having the seal of the living God. He called out in a loud voice to the four angels who had been given power to harm the land and the sea: 'Do not harm the land or the sea or the trees until we put a seal on the foreheads of the servants of our God'" (Rev. 7:1–3). This sealing can only point to divine protection from judgment.

## Divine Protection from Mere Wind?

Over and over in Scripture, we see havoc that is caused by an east wind, and because the angel in our text comes from the east, we could simply accept this prophecy at face value and take it literally. But first let's build a physical model in our mind's eye and envision how being sealed by the Almighty God could affect those who receive his seal. Let's consider two men standing on the same street in a major city; one of them has the seal of God upon him and the other does not, and the wind is blowing extremely hard. Will the one who has God's seal be affected by the wind any less than the other man? Is literal wind the destructive force that God will protect his faithful from? Probably not—after all the word usage in Revelation usually has a figurative meaning.

*Wind* throughout Scripture is associated with a spirit, or force, like when the "sound like the blowing of a violent wind came from heaven and filled the whole house where"[103] people were praying. Could the first trumpet be dealing with a spiritual force—possibly an evil wind? Again, let's look to the Old Testament for a possible example: this next text depicts God's people when they were worried about a possible conquest: "Ahaz and his people were shaken, as the trees of the forest are shaken by the wind" (Isa. 7:2). This text even likened people to "the trees of the forest." This is noteworthy because trees were mentioned in the trumpet judgment. Please notice these people were "shaken," meaning they were terribly frightened—the Bible verse makes no mention of any storm looming; it was a warring faction of Israel that was ominous. People at the end of time who have forsaken the knowledge of God will be spiritually and emotionally shaken by the coming conquest of God's Christ, and "like the wind their sins will sweep them away."[104] Yet those who are in fellowship with the Lord have no need to fear.

This next text is an end-time prophecy: it fits perfectly into our time frame and speaks of the coming low moral condition of the earth. "The earth reels like a drunkard, it sways like a hut in the wind; so heavy upon it is the guilt of its rebellion that it falls—never to rise again" (Isa. 24:20). Wind was mentioned in that text. In the last days, the wind of God's judgment will blow upon our troubled world, yet the earth will not literally fall—these are figurative statements.

Speaking of one of the tribes of Israel, it is written, "Ephraim feeds on the wind; he pursues the east wind all day and multiplies lies and violence" (Hos. 12:1). Surely the wind is likened to a negative force in that passage. Is it possible that the wind that blows near the end of time could be an illustration of "multiplies lies and violence"? In another Bible verse where wind is mentioned it reads, "May they be like chaff before the wind, with the angel of the Lord driving them away; may their path be dark and slippery, with the angel of the Lord pursuing them" (Ps. 35:5–6). Seeing that the "angel of the Lord" is shown chasing after the wicked, the word usage points to the word *wind* representing a driving or pursuing force. None of these texts is speaking of a literal wind.

Now please don't misunderstand the point of my arguments. I would be the last man on earth to say there won't be terrifying winds before Christ returns. What I am saying is, God is not going to seal us from mere wind—the protection He gives His faithful ones is protection from coming judgment that will sweep through our world like an east wind—judgment of a spiritual nature, which is far more devastating.

## The First Trumpet Sounds

"The first angel sounded his trumpet, and there came hail and fire mixed with blood, and it was hurled down upon the earth. A third of the earth was burned up, a third of the trees were burned up, and all the green grass was burned up" (Rev. 8:7). If we were to take the meaning of this last text literally, from a purely scientific standpoint, we might surmise that hail and fire mixed with blood was the result of a nuclear conflict—that's a good possibility. If one-third of earth's trees burned, the amount of smoke this would create and the amount of carbon dioxide it would produce would indeed cause famine on a major scale. This burning could also account for the moon turning red and the sun withdrawing its light, but wait! This type of devastation may be a little too much at this point in our timeline. Evidently we still have a year left before Armageddon. So again, we should consider that the word usage in our text might be figurative.

Let's ask the question, what might hail and fire mixed with blood represent—spiritual warfare? This first trumpet will probably have more to do with the continued deception and apostasy of men and women rather than the literal destruction of vegetation.

## A Symbolic Application

Let's consider the part of the verse where it reads, "All the green grass was burned up." Why only the green grass? Why not the multitude of grass that is mature and still standing, about to be harvested? And what about the wheat and barley grass that is cut and baled, yet still lying in the fields? Maybe we're not talking about grass at all. Let's ask the question: could this term "green" in prophecy be speaking of people with shallow roots who have turned from the knowledge of God? The Bible says, "like the grass they will soon wither, like green plants they will soon die away" (Ps. 37:2).

Let's look at the part of the verse where it reads, "A third of the trees were burned up." In Revelation—speaking of Satan, where he is illustrated as a red dragon—it's written, "His tail swept a third of the stars out of the sky and flung them to the earth" (Rev. 12:4). The time frame when "a third" of these stars hit the earth is during Antichrist's regime. Because the term "his tail" is used (speaking of the dragon), this could refer to a time near the end of his reign. If these stars falling depict men and women falling from the faith, then the trees that are burned up may represent people as well. One thing is certain: When the first trumpet sounds, the war in the spirit will escalate. God is going to seal us from harm, yet the forces we shall be protected from are far more deadly than wind.

## The Second Trumpet Sounds

"The second angel sounded his trumpet, and something like a huge mountain, all ablaze, was thrown into the sea. A third of the sea turned into blood, a third of the living creatures in the sea died, and a third of the ships were destroyed" (Rev. 8:8–9). Before we decide if this text should be taken literally or if it has a figurative meaning, let's look at the word usage where we find *sea* elsewhere in the same book. The word *sea* is found 26 times in Revelation. Here are a few examples:

1. "Therefore rejoice, you heavens and you who dwell in them! But woe to the earth and the sea, because the devil has gone down to you! He is filled with fury, because he knows that his time is short" (Rev. 12:12).
2. "And the dragon stood on the shore of the sea" (Rev. 12:18).
3. "And I saw a beast coming out of the sea" (Rev. 13:1).

Within prophetic Scripture the *earth* can represent political strongholds while the *sea* can be an illustration of multitudes of people, languages, and nations.[105] The expression *sea creatures* is used in the Bible in reference to men, as in this passage, "You have made men like fish in the sea, like sea creatures that have no ruler" (Hab. 1:14). The terms, *ships* and *captains* can also have figurative meanings. For example, Jesus is the captain[106] of our salvation.

The devil's fury will not be focused upon a literal sea—his woes will affect multitudes of people, of different languages, consisting of many nations. Many among us will be looking for natural plagues coming in the days ahead and will fail to notice the more subtle deception Satan will be using. What we believe and what we profess and to whom we hold our allegiance is what the devil and his angels will be attacking. Their fury will be aimed at our faith in God.

A mountain on fire being hurled into the sea is speaking of Satan's governmental forces impacting the nations, affecting multitudes and eventually burning out and coming to an end. "'I am against you, O destroying mountain, you who destroy the whole earth,' declares the Lord. 'I will stretch out my hand against you, roll you off the cliffs, and make you a burned-out mountain'" (Jer. 51:25). This mountain that the Lord rolled off the cliffs—presumably into the sea—in time past was the Babylonian Empire. The same language used in Jeremiah illustrating how Babylon of old would be destroyed is also used in Revelation concerning modern Babylon's coming destruction. Ancient Babylon did fall and its mountain burned out just as prophesied—the Lord cast its burning mountain into the sea, figuratively speaking.

However, no one on earth saw a literal mountain descend into the ocean; that wasn't necessary to fulfill the prophecy. Jesus said, "I tell you the truth, if anyone says to this mountain, 'Go, throw yourself into the sea,' and does not doubt in his heart but believes that what he says will happen, it will be done for him" (Mark 11:23). Christ was speaking in figurative language. If we are looking for a real mountain to be cast into the sea during the days of Revelation's trumpet judgments, we will be missing out on the real wonder. Jesus Christ was talking about throwing down the powers of darkness and the spiritual forces of evil in heavenly realms—this "mountain" in Scripture is Satan's kingdom.

The creatures in the sea who die are men and women who die spiritually due to the strong pressure this mountain imposes upon their unstable faith. The irony is, part of their lack of faith could be due to a misunderstanding of the Bible. After all, if they knew what to look for in the time of deception and how to prepare for it, why would they die in the sea?

## The Third Trumpet Sounds

"The third angel sounded his trumpet, and a great star, blazing like a torch, fell from the sky on a third of the rivers and on the springs of water—the name of the star is Wormwood. A third of the waters turned bitter, and many people died from the waters that had become bitter" (Rev. 8:10–11). A popular theory about this plague, taken from a literal viewpoint, is that the star named Wormwood in our text is depicting nuclear material polluting our fresh water supply. This is a good theory; "Chernobyl" translated into English spells Wormwood. Russia's nuclear reactor by the same name once leaked massive amounts of radiation. It's likely the earth will see contamination from radiation again before Armageddon from a number of sources, including possible tactical nuclear exchanges in eastern nations. Yet this text is crying out a figurative meaning, and here are some reasons why: This great star falls on rivers and streams and one-third of the earth's water is affected! From a strictly geological standpoint, it would be impossible for the star to affect only fresh water, because on a scale of this magnitude the oceans would also be impacted.

This star has a name. In the same book, speaking of a different trumpet plague, we see another "star that had fallen from the sky to the earth. The star was given the key to the shaft of the Abyss." (Rev. 9:1). This star also is called "the angel of the Abyss, whose name in Hebrew is Abaddon, and in Greek, Apollyon"[107] or in English, Satan.

We should note that the star of the Abyss—Satan—also fell from the sky just like Wormwood did. Bitter waters in Scripture are illustrations of spiritual deception, which can lead to spiritual death.

## What Do the Prophets Say about Rivers and Streams?

Jesus cried, "'If anyone is thirsty, let him come to me and drink. Whoever believes in me, as the Scripture has said, streams of living water will flow from within him.' By this he meant the Spirit" (John 7:37–39). Streams of fresh water depict the Spirit of God. In the last days, Satan and his whole host will pollute our spiritual environment. This is what the divine protection is for—without God's seal on our forehead, we would be vulnerable to the bitter waters during these trumpet plagues. Why a seal in the forehead? This place on our body could be symbolic of where we hold our knowledge. A wise man seeking knowledge will find it; that is a sure promise from the Word. Knowledge of God's Word is the key to surviving these plagues. Satan wouldn't be satisfied with just harming people's bodies—he wants to thwart Christ's victory where it hurts the most: in the faith of men.

## The Fourth Trumpet Sounds

> The fourth angel sounded his trumpet, and a third of the sun was struck, a third of the moon, and a third of the stars, so that a third of them turned dark. A third of the day was without light, and also a third of the night. (Rev. 8:12)

This trumpet plague is speaking of a great loss of light. Our source of light, "the sun," that which reflects its light, "the moon," and even the hours of the day, "time itself," will be lacking in light by one-third. Before we look for a symbolic application to this lack of light, let's look for a natural physical explanation.

A theory has sprung up over the years explaining how a huge celestial object will strike the earth and that this object's impact will speed up the earth's rotation by one-third. However, there are problems with this theory. From a scientific standpoint, any object with enough mass and velocity to speed earth's rotation by one-third after impact would also shatter the earth's thin crust, causing liquid magma to spill out over most of the globe—killing all life on the planet.

Looking into Bible prophecy in the books of Ezekiel[108] and Daniel,[109] during the last days before Armageddon, we see a list of nations—some protesting the siege upon Jerusalem and others who are engaging in it. Yet if a large object had hit the earth and sped up its rotation by one-third, why are these nations still in existence? Even if the object just hit the ocean, it would still destroy most life on the planet. Also, the narrative in these books between these warring nations seems too calm if such a catastrophic event had occurred. For those simple reasons, let's look in the Word for a figurative explanation.

## Darkness in Prophetic Scripture

It will be earth's darkest hour before the dawn arrives. All the forces of evil, knowing this is their last hurrah, will be lashing out at everything they can. Satan is about to be cast into a dungeon. His whole entourage is about to be removed from power. The opportunity to deceive man and wreak havoc is coming to an end. So they will try to spoil what's left of their domain; they will initiate a scorched-earth policy and try to burn what remains. "Before them fire devours, behind them a flame blazes. Before them the land is like the garden of Eden, behind them, a desert waste—nothing escapes them. They have the appearance of horses; they gallop along like cavalry. With a noise like that of chariots they leap over the mountaintops, like a crackling fire consuming stubble, like a mighty army drawn up for battle. . . . Before them the earth shakes, the sky trembles, the sun and moon are darkened, and the stars no longer shine" (Joel 2:3–5 and 10).

> Therefore night will come over you, without visions, and darkness, without divination. The sun will set for the prophets, and the day will go dark for them. The seers will be ashamed and the diviners disgraced. They will all cover their faces because there is no answer from God. (Mic. 3:6–7)

# Chapter 7

# AN INVASION OF LOCUSTS

Hear this, you elders; listen, all who live in the land. Has anything like this ever happened in your days or in the days of your forefathers? Tell it to your children, and let your children tell it to their children, and their children to the next generation. What the locust swarm has left the great locusts have eaten; what the great locusts have left the young locusts have eaten; what the young locusts have left other locusts have eaten. Wake up, you drunkards, and weep! Wail, all you drinkers of wine; wail because of the new wine, for it has been snatched from your lips. A nation has invaded my land, powerful and without number; it has the teeth of a lion, the fangs of a lioness. It has laid waste my vines and ruined my fig trees. It has stripped off their bark and thrown it away, leaving their branches white. Mourn like a virgin in sackcloth grieving for the husband of her youth. Grain offerings and drink offerings are cut off from the house of the LORD. The priests are in mourning, those who minister before the LORD. The fields are ruined, the ground is dried up; the grain is destroyed, the new wine is dried up, the oil fails. Despair, you farmers . . . (Joel 1:2–11)

What comes to mind when we think of locusts? Good things? Probably not. Locusts are part of the curse that man suffers. As they swarm they look hideous, like a dark plague moving through the air, making a buzzing noise and leaving destruction in their wake. When locusts swarm into the farmland, they devour everything in their path.

Envision a farmer's wife looking out the window into the wheat fields, seeing a cloud of locusts approaching, and then crying out to her husband, "Honey, the locusts are coming, and there's millions of them." Do you think her husband would reply, "That's nice, dear"? Not in a million years! Locusts are a terror to farmers. They devour the wheat and corn.

Throughout Scripture there are illustrations in nature to teach us. Wheat[110] and corn in the natural fields of this earth depict people throughout their formative years as they develop spiritually. Locusts[111] are physical representations of a spiritual design,[112] too—an evil design. Figuratively speaking, they devour men: this is exactly what we see the locusts of Revelation do. We see them pushing through the spiritual veil into our physical realm to torment mankind.

"As I watched, I heard an eagle that was flying in midair call out in a loud voice: 'Woe! Woe! Woe to the inhabitants of the earth, because of the trumpet blasts about to be sounded by the other three angels!'" (Rev. 8:13). The locusts are released with the trumpet blast of the fifth angel. "The fifth angel sounded his trumpet, and I saw a star that had fallen from the sky to the earth. The star was given the key to the shaft of the Abyss" (Rev. 9:1). As we have seen, this star falling from heaven to earth is Satan; he is allowed to open up a pit containing hideous beasts called locusts: "When he opened the Abyss, smoke rose from it like the smoke from a gigantic furnace. The sun and sky were darkened by the smoke from the Abyss" (Rev. 9:2).

## An Invasion of Locusts

This verse has connotations of spiritual darkness. As the angel opens this pit, smoke comes out and the sun is darkened. As we have noted, the sun in prophetic Scripture represents Jesus Christ in his Father's glory: "But for you who revere my name, the sun of righteousness will rise with healing in its wings" (Mal. 4:2).

The sun is our source of light. Demons blind men's minds, keeping them in darkness—they keep men from the Sun of righteousness who is at their heart's door waiting to heal them. Nevertheless, God can deliver the repentant man from gross darkness no matter how far the devil has brought him.

"And out of the smoke locusts came down upon the earth and were given power like that of scorpions of the earth" (Rev. 9:3). The key to understanding what these locusts are is this: They "were given power." The horsemen of the Apocalypse were also given power. Satan claimed that the power over the kingdoms of the world was delivered unto him. In the book of Job, "The LORD said to Satan, 'Very well, then, everything he [Job] has is in your hands'" (Job 1:12b).

The locusts "were told not to harm the grass of the earth or any plant or tree, but only those people who did not have the seal of God on their foreheads" (Rev. 9:4). As we have seen previously, God seals 144,000 children of Israel on their foreheads with His very name before any trumpets sound, protecting all those who make up Israel (Christians) from this demon plague.

The locusts "were not given power to kill men, but only to torture mankind for five months. And the agony they will suffer is like that of the sting of a scorpion when it strikes a man. During these days men will seek death, but will not find it; they will long to die, but death will elude them" (Rev. 9:5–6, author's paraphrase). The torment from the locusts will be so severe, many men would rather die than endure the pain.

"The locusts looked like horses prepared for battle. On their heads they wore something like crowns of gold, and their faces resembled human faces" (Rev. 9:7). The twenty-four elders of Revelation 4 cast their crowns before the Lord, and the living creatures of that same chapter have faces like men; they also have wings. The twenty-four elders and the living creatures are symbolic of the sons of God in their glorified state. These locusts are a symbolic illustration of angels in a fallen state.

Please notice that these demons were viewed as "horses prepared for battle." This illustration is similar to the four horses of the Apocalypse. These locusts wear gold crowns, as do God's glorified sons. Therefore the locusts have been in heaven at one time; the crowns they have tell of the divinity they once shared with God. In fact, the crowns point to them being sons of God just like Satan, whose fellow spirits ride like horsemen through the earth, bringing destruction and death.

"Their hair was like women's hair, and their teeth were like lions' teeth. They had breastplates like breastplates of iron, and the sound of their wings was like the thundering of many horses and chariots rushing into battle" (Rev. 9:8–9). The saying, "They had breastplates like breastplates of iron," means this is an illustration that should not be taken literally; these creatures do not have literal breastplates of iron. This illustration of armor shows that these locusts are geared for battle. "They had tails and stings like scorpions, and in their tails they had power to torment people . . ." (Rev. 9:10).

The symbolism depicting locusts in Revelation is pointing to demonic activity. Millions of demonic spirits will be swarming after receiving permission from the courts of heaven to torment men. "They are spirits of demons performing miraculous signs, and they go out to the kings of the whole world, to gather them for the battle on the great day of God Almighty" (Rev. 16:14).

Christians will not be dodging missiles at the time of the first woe. Building hardened bunkers is not what will protect men from the woes in this prophecy. This plague has to do with a spiritual, invisible, battle involving an enemy rarely seen.

## Woe No. 2

> The first woe is past; two other woes are yet to come.
>
> The sixth angel sounded his trumpet, and I heard a voice coming from the horns of the golden altar that is before God. It said to the sixth angel who had the trumpet, "Release the four angels who are bound at the great river Euphrates." And the four angels who had been kept ready for this very hour and day and month and year were released to kill a third of mankind. The number of the mounted troops was two hundred million. I heard their number.
>
> The horses and riders I saw in my vision looked like this: Their breastplates were fiery red, dark blue, and yellow as sulfur. The heads of the horses resembled the heads of lions, and out of their mouths came fire, smoke and sulfur. A third of mankind was killed by the three plagues of fire, smoke and sulfur that came out of their mouths. The power of the horses was in their mouths and in their tails; for their tails were like snakes, having heads with which they inflict injury. (Rev. 9:12–19)

## Highly Figurative Language

This is highly figurative language. The sixth angel is blowing a trumpet, a voice is heard from the horns of the golden altar, four angels are loosed from the great river Euphrates, then we have a vivid description of an army of horsemen. While John undoubtedly saw these things, we must keep in mind that these are only symbols pointing to a more profound meaning.

## The Mystery of the Altar Explained

The Temple in the Old Testament was a house where God dwelled. Obviously, that earthly temple was only an illustration of a spiritual design—even the heavenly temple is merely a facsimile that God is using to teach us. An altar with four horns is not unusual: when God commanded Moses to build the Tabernacle (which was a portable temple), he also told him to make several instruments that would be used within. Among these instruments were seven golden lampstands and an altar with four horns. We have already noted that each of the lampstands represents a church, such as the church of Laodicea, consisting of multitudes of people. Because the temple's seven-branched lampstand represents seven assemblies of God's faithful, we should seriously consider this heavenly altar might also represent multitudes of faithful men, women, and children as well.

## The Shadow of the Altar in Heaven

In the days Israel was traveling in the wilderness, God commanded Moses:

> Build an altar of acacia wood, three cubits high; it is to be square, five cubits long and five cubits wide. Make a horn at each of the four corners, so that the horns and the altar are of one piece, and overlay the altar with bronze. Make all its utensils of bronze—its pots to remove the ashes, and its shovels, sprinkling bowls, meat forks and firepans. Make a grating for it, a bronze network, and make a bronze ring at each of the four corners of the network. Put it under the ledge of the altar so that it is halfway up the altar. Make poles of acacia wood for the altar and overlay them with bronze. The poles are to be inserted into the rings so they will be on two sides of the altar when it is carried. Make the altar hollow, out of boards. It is to be made just as you were shown on the mountain. (Exod. 7:1–8)

The Hebrew word used for "horn" in our text is *qeren* from the primary root *qaran*, meaning "to shoot out horns"; a horn as projecting; a corner (of the altar); a peak (of the mountain); figurative of power.

An animal's power is in its horns. Horns also grow. They "shoot out." Throughout Scripture this word *horn* is used in correspondence with people. Here are a few examples: "I will cut off the horns of all the wicked, but the horns of the righteous will be lifted up" (Ps. 75:10). "My faithful love will be with him, and through my name his horn will be exalted" (Ps. 89:24).

Revelation's Lamb has seven horns;[113] Revelation's beast has ten.[114] It's written that the beast's horns are crowned and they are ten kings.[115] Kings brandish power over nations, especially in time of war; kingdoms also shoot out and encompass the earth. This is what the book of Revelation is about—war over earth's domain between the armies of heaven[116] and the Antichrist's *evil*[117] empire.

Yet how can an altar's horns illustrate power or shooting out, as in the lineage of men and women? Living things die in front of an altar and are consumed by fire upon one. Death is what an altar is about. This altar's four horns are symbolic of death on a worldwide scale. Looking from a natural perspective, a dying man is powerless and no longer able to produce seed.

However, spiritually speaking, this is not the case—a dying man's body is a seed. "The body that is sown is perishable, it is raised imperishable; it is sown in dishonor, it is raised in glory; it is sown in weakness, it is raised in power" (1 Cor. 14: 42–43). Speaking of a dying man, Jesus said, "Unless a kernel of wheat falls to the ground and dies, it remains only a single seed" (John 12:24).

## Souls under the Altar

What significance does an altar have? It implies sacrifice. In the book of Revelation it also implies martyrdom—the killing of the innocent. The Apostle John "saw under the altar the souls of those who had been slain because of the word of God and the testimony they had maintained. They called out in a loud voice, 'How long, Sovereign Lord, holy and true, until you judge the inhabitants of the earth and avenge our blood?' Then each of them was given a white robe, and they were told to wait a little longer, until the number of their fellow servants and brothers who were to be killed as they had been was completed" (Rev. 6:9–11).

What John saw was martyrs throughout history—these saints were unwilling to deny their faith at any price, and they were calling out for vengeance. God told them to wait for the sacrifice of their brothers and sisters to come under Antichrist's regime as we have read: "wait a little longer" for the rest[118] to be killed. This huge crowd of martyrs is one facet of God's Church.

## A Typological Analogy of Sacrifice

During the Old Testament dispensation, the bodies of goats and lambs were consumed by fire on the altar, and the smoke from the sacrifice would well up as a sweet savor to God. However, without people's faith in the covenant, the ceremony would have meant nothing and God would not have been pleased. God is not interested in the sacrifices of animals—He never has been. What God desires and what these sacrifices represent has to do with heartfelt commitments from His faithful children. In one sense, our flesh is to be consumed by fire daily so that only the gold (deity) remains. It's our lives that need to be laid upon the altar in an act of sacrifice to God every day, not some animal's flesh! When our lower nature is burned away (figuratively speaking), what comes up from the ashes is a consecrated soul. In like manner during the resurrection we will see that the same thing has occurred—our lower nature along with all of our imperfections will have been purged in death.

## The Prayers of All the Saints

> Another angel, who had a golden censer, came and stood at the altar. He was given much incense to offer, with the prayers of all the saints, on the golden altar before the throne. The smoke of the incense, together with the prayers of the saints, went up before God from the angel's hand. Then the angel took the censer, filled it with fire from the altar, and hurled it on the earth." (Rev. 8:3–5)

What is beautiful about this passage is that the altar is shown before the throne. The spirit is teaching us that God cares about His faithful children. He rejoices over the faith of those who would rather die than deny His name. They are in His presence day and night and He hearkens to their pleas—many of the final plagues in Revelation are a direct result of the martyrs' cries. As John saw the final bowls of God's wrath being poured out, he "heard the altar respond: 'Yes, Lord God Almighty, true and just are your judgments'" (Rev. 16:7).

A voice from the altar sets the destroying angels in motion, telling an angel to release four angels who are bound at the great river Euphrates. And the four angels were released to kill a third of mankind. Once more, I believe the number four in our text is pointing to a worldwide application to some aspects of this plague. Otherwise, we might ask, why would only four angels participate in an event of this scale? While it may be possible for merely four angels to stir up millions of human troops, we should consider that this is the devil's last season to wreak havoc on the earth before Christ comes. He is determined to destroy all that which Jesus is going to obtain by succession. It seems ironic that out of the millions of fallen angels that are hell-bent for destruction, only four would participate. What are the rest of them doing?

We see that two hundred million horsemen are involved in this plague. One popular teaching on this subject is that these horsemen represent the Chinese military because China can muster an army of this size. However, I'm not so sure this vision is one of human forces. These horses are identical to the locusts that come from the bottomless pit and also the four horses that come from the presence of the Lord. It's very likely the forces John spoke of here are Satanic influences behind human factions.

Chapter  8

# THE FINAL WOE

> I saw in heaven another great and marvelous sign: seven angels with the seven last plagues—last, because with them God's wrath is completed (Rev. 15:1).

Could this wrath of God, ending with the battle of Armageddon, be the "hour of trial"[119] that Christ promised he would keep his faithful from? Apparently, the Rapture of the church, which is called the "first resurrection" in Scripture, takes place right before these plagues pour down.

All of heaven is looking forward to this resurrection, for with it dawns a new age. At this time, the promise of the Creator will be expressed in His creation. We will come into the pattern[120] for which we were designed. Mankind will come into the image of Christ.

## The Trumpet Sounds and the Voice Commands—Come Up Here

As the seventh angel raises his trumpet to his lips and sounds it, a great voice from heaven cries out the command, "Come up here." Out of the dust, millions of souls are raised and begin to ascend; then we who are still alive become as light as a feather. As we take on the wings of eagles, we fly to our heavenly nests.

As we are transformed from this earthbound body into a glorified form, instantly we understand where we're going, our thoughts are focused, our senses are sharp; as we stream through space, we're overjoyed. We are standing on the threshold of eternity.

There's no oppression in this realm—we're encompassed with love from all sides. The victory is ours. The curse is far behind. Death no longer reigns. We are free. As we finish up the inaugural feasts and celebrations, our attention shifts back to earth, where Satan and his entourage have been stirring up trouble.

## Angels, Pour Out Your Bowls

Jesus leads us to the house of God where seven bowls lie waiting. Stepping out from the smoke of the incense, seven angels appear. "Then I heard a loud voice from the temple saying to the seven angels, 'Go, pour out the seven bowls of God's wrath on the earth'" (Rev. 16:1).

As the suffering escalates during the final weeks before Christ returns, it will be like hell on earth. Some may wonder how a loving God could be so cruel. This is not the case—it's out of mercy that these plagues fall. If God had decided to kill the wicked instantaneously, that would be far less humane. Our loving Father is reaching His hand out, even until earth's final hour. Some will come to their senses during this time, just like back in Noah's day when they saw the ark rising above the waters of judgment. Back then, multitudes reflected upon Noah's message, repented, and found salvation.

## A Testimony Rejected

However, God has kept the light from shining too brightly upon the minds and hearts of the obstinate malefactors. Nothing good[121] will come from this trial for them; going through these days without opening their hearts will only add to their judgment: for the wicked, this will be a day of punishment.

By this time, the population of earth will have heard the gospel warning from many sources, because through his collective body (the church), Christ will have warned them. The Creator made a provision in his plan for people to find the door of Christ and escape the wrath to come, but they ignored his message. Therefore Christ will trample them as one who treads in the wine. It is written, "I have trodden the winepress alone; from the nations no one was with me. I trampled them in my anger and trod them down in my wrath; their blood spattered my garments, and I stained all my clothing. For the day of vengeance was in my heart, and the year of my redemption has come. I trampled the nations in my anger; in my wrath I made them drunk and poured their blood on the ground" (Isa. 63:3–4 and 6).

## The First Bowl—Painful Sores

> The first angel went and poured out his bowl on the land, and ugly and painful sores broke out on the people who had the mark of the beast and worshiped his image. (Rev. 16:2)

This plague is spiritual in nature: it affects only people who had the mark of the beast and worshiped his image. As we have noted before, the terms *land* and *sea*, which are used multiple times in Revelation, represent multitudes of people and nations in political and religious realms. This plague is not aimed at the soil we walk on—people are the target of this woe.

In the last days the torment from the underworld and the judgment from God will transcend spiritual bounds—and will cross over into our physical realm. There's little doubt people will be stricken with boils and see the welts rise up as the locusts are stinging them. However, the most oppressive torment which man will endure is torment of the mind. Spiritual torment is coming. Like in a nightmare which one suffers, not understanding they are dreaming, people will suffer greatly with unknown forces haunting their imagination.

> Awake, awake! Rise up, O Jerusalem, you who have drunk from the hand of the Lord the cup of his wrath, you who have drained to its dregs the goblet that makes men stagger. These double calamities have come upon you—who can comfort you?—ruin and destruction, famine and sword—who can console you? Your sons have fainted; they lie at the head of every street, like antelope caught in a net. They are filled with the wrath of the Lord and the rebuke of your God. Therefore hear this, you afflicted one, made drunk, but not with wine." (Isa. 51:17 and 19–21)

## The Second Bowl—Blood and Death in the Sea

The second angel poured out his bowl on the sea, and it turned into blood like that of a dead man, and every living thing in the sea died" (Rev. 16:3). This bowl plague is similar to the plague accompanying the second trumpet, yet instead of just one-third of the creatures in the sea dying, with this plague every living thing dies.

Earth's natural sea is a vast body of water that mingles with many other bodies of water; it's heavily salted, making it undrinkable. This water holds no nourishment for mankind unless it's purified. From a spiritual viewpoint, the sea represents all the world's religions outside of Christ—religions that have been salted with false teaching.

At this time, the one world order established by the Antichrist will have married many false religions into a one-world prostitute religion. This false church, which is depicted as both a woman and a great city in Revelation, will come under spiritual judgment. It's written concerning her, "Come out of her, my people, so that you will not share in her sins, so that you will not receive any of her plagues; for her sins are piled up to heaven, and God has remembered her crimes. Give back to her as she has given; pay her back double for what she has done. Mix her a double portion from her own cup" (Rev. 18:4–6).

The Lord isn't going to kill every living thing in earth's natural oceans. The fish in the sea aren't rebelling against their Creator—man is. This is a spiritual judgment upon all the men, women, and children who have rejected the true God and His Christ and have served the false christ instead. It's written, speaking of Antichrist's world religion, Mystery Babylon: "By your magic spell all the nations were led astray. In her was found the blood of prophets and of the saints, and of all who have been killed on the earth" (Rev. 18:23–24).

## The Third Bowl—Fresh Water Turns to Blood

> The third angel poured out his bowl on the rivers and springs of water, and they became blood. Then I heard the angel in charge of the waters say: "You are just in these judgments, you who are and who were, the Holy One, because you have so judged; for they have shed the blood of your saints and prophets, and you have given them blood to drink as they deserve." (Rev. 16:4–6)

This plague is figurative of judgment on a major scale. Many parallels are drawn from water in Scripture—fresh water is the wellspring of life. Rivers and springs depict the spirit of God, which nourishes our spirits. Yet with this final plague, the spirit, which once sustained man, is bringing death to all the people who have sinned against it.

## The Fourth Bowl—Crank Up the Heat

> The fourth angel poured out his bowl on the sun, and the sun was given power to scorch people with fire. They were seared by the intense heat and they cursed the name of God, who had control over these plagues, but they refused to repent and glorify him. (Rev. 16:8–9)

We have already noted that the sun in Bible prophecy depicts Jesus Christ in glory. While we could continue to pursue a figurative explanation of this and the following plagues (understanding that some figurative analogies do apply), I believe we would be missing the message to ignore a physical application. There's too much evidence in the Scriptures indicating that the natural forces of our environment will run to extremes. It's my understanding that at this point in time, man will endure severe physical suffering from natural forces.

It's very likely that from the beginning of Creation, the hand of God has set these coming events in motion. For example: in the days of Noah before the flood came, the earth was a ticking bomb. Many scholars believe that earthquakes and subsequent volcanoes salted the upper atmosphere with particles on which water vapor condensed and formed rain. This water vapor canopy[122] was unseen to the naked eye—the people of Noah's time had no idea it existed—yet it was looming over their heads every day. When the rain fell, bringing down that blanket of water, it destroyed that generation. God used natural forces to carry out the great plague of Noah's day.

In this generation, earth's population may have a ticking bomb looming above in the form of the sun. Modern science holds that our sun is too small to explode as in the case of a supernova. What it can do as it ends its lifespan is shift into a nova condition, expanding in size and increasing in temperature, which would cause intense heat upon earth. If the sun began to go into the early stages of a nova, that could explain the nature of the fourth bowl plague. It would also provide a sign in the heavens above, as it is written, "There will be great earthquakes, famines and pestilences in various places, and fearful events and great signs from heaven" (Luke 21:11). However, anything is possible with God; we should not rule out the possibility that some plagues may be a result of divine intervention.

## The Fifth Bowl—Darkness

> The fifth angel poured out his bowl on the throne of the beast, and his kingdom was plunged into darkness. Men gnawed their tongues in agony and cursed the God of heaven because of their pains and their sores, but they refused to repent of what they had done. (Rev. 16:10–11)

The darkness to come will be far worse for mankind than what Egypt suffered. It's recorded in Scripture[123] that the lack of light they endured merely obscured people's sight. Egypt's darkness was merely a physical model of the spiritual darkness to come. Armageddon will be man's darkest hour: The sun shall withdraw its light and then the end will come. Revelation paints a picture of men staggering around in gross darkness because they have rejected Christ. Revelation's pages contain images of underlying forces tormenting men and women and influencing them to accomplish their will.

> The coming of the lawless one will be in accordance with the work of Satan displayed in all kinds of counterfeit miracles, signs and wonders, and in every sort of evil that deceives those who are perishing. They perish because they refused to love the truth and so be saved. For this reason God sends them a powerful delusion so that they will believe the lie. (Thess. 2:9–11)

Let's look at the crucifixion of Jesus for an example of the dark hour to come:

> From the sixth hour until the ninth hour darkness came over all the land. About the ninth hour Jesus cried out in a loud voice, "*Eloi, Eloi, lama sabachthani?*"—which means, "My God, my God, why have you forsaken me?" And when Jesus had cried out again in a loud voice, he gave up his spirit. At that moment the curtain of the temple was torn in two from top to bottom. The earth shook and the rocks split. The tombs broke open and the bodies of many holy people who had died were raised to life. They came out of the tombs, and after Jesus' resurrection they went into the holy city and appeared to many people. When the centurion and those with him who were guarding Jesus saw the earthquake and all that had happened, they were terrified, and exclaimed, "Surely he was the Son of God." (Matt. 27:45, 50–54)

Tremendous signs were brought forth, and they all occurred during and as a result of the Savior's death. Some in the crowd repented at the final hour. The earth had shaken; the sun had withdrawn its light. People were raised from the graves. Many had witnessed the heavy curtain in the Temple tear from the top down (this was a sign from heaven), meaning from this day on, the most holy place in the Temple (the place where God dwelled) was open to man through the sacrifice of His Christ.

It's interesting to note the different reactions among men and women who witnessed Christ's death; for some, their lives were never the same. As they watched him die, they beat their chests in remorse, realizing they had put to death their long-awaited Redeemer. Others simply went about business as usual, closing their eyes to the strange darkness, earthquakes, and other manifestations. These people allowed a veil[124] to cover their hearts, easing their consciences.

## The Sixth Bowl—Prepare the Way to Armageddon

> The sixth angel poured out his bowl on the great river Euphrates, and its water was dried up to prepare the way for the kings from the East. Then I saw three evil spirits that looked like frogs; they came out of the mouth of the dragon, out of the mouth of the beast and out of the mouth of the false prophet. They are spirits of demons performing miraculous signs, and they go out to the kings of the whole world, to gather them for the battle on the great day of God Almighty. Then they gathered the kings together to the place that in Hebrew is called Armageddon. (Rev. 16: 12–14, 16)

The Euphrates River runs through Syria and Iraq; Iran is to the east of it and Russia is to the far north. Any army coming from the north or the east would have to cross the Euphrates before it could attack Jerusalem, and those coming from the far north would have to dogleg to the east as they approached Israel.

Now we need to ask the question, is it physically possible that the great river Euphrates could run dry during the last seven weeks before Armageddon? Personally, I am convinced this is the case. Some may wonder why we should now lean toward a literal interpretation of a passage in Revelation when up until this point, we have interpreted nearly every verse figuratively. Here's why:

It's very likely that in a book written in symbols, there may be some conventional narrative. For example, in other places in Scripture, such as when reading the parables of Christ, there are cases where the meaning of the parable is given. I cannot see any convincing symbolic application to this prophecy. From a strictly geographical standpoint, it makes sense—armies coming from the east would have to cross that river just like the Scripture expresses.

And this understanding coincides with Old Testament prophecies showing that Iran, Turkey, and Russia will come against Jerusalem in the last days.

> Charge, O horses! Drive furiously, O charioteers! March on, O warriors—men of Cush and Put who carry shields, men of Lydia who draw the bow. But that day belongs to the Lord, the LORD Almighty—a day of vengeance, for vengeance on his foes. The sword will devour till it is satisfied, till it has quenched its thirst with blood. For the Lord, the LORD Almighty, will offer sacrifice in the land of the north by the River Euphrates. (Jer. 46:9–10)

This last passage was originally written about a war between Nebuchadnezzar, king of Babylon, and Egypt, yet we are not taking the passage out of context by using it as a reference text for Armageddon. Aside from the true saying "History repeats itself," we may also note that many Old Testament prophecies start with a limited historical application and then end up speaking of the end of time.

## The Judgment upon Israel

Israel has killed every prophet God has sent to them, including John the Baptist and Jesus Christ. Prophets shall be sent at the end of the age, and these, too, will be killed. Israel will choose a hard path with God and a hard path they shall receive.

Please don't misunderstand—God loves Israel. Nevertheless, Israel is God's covenant people, and part of the covenant which was handed to them calls for a divine curse when they walk away from Him. At this point in time, Israel will have wandered further away from God than at any previous time. Israel will have accepted the Antichrist and entered into a covenant with him. Israel will have joined hands with Satan through the policies he set in place.

The Antichrist will show his true colors as he abandons the covenant people (Israel) and defiles their Temple. The religious peace between Israel and the surrounding nations which the new world order had maintained will be shattered at this time. The well-rounded Bible student understands that God often uses wicked forces to bring about his judgments: "The beast and the ten horns you saw will hate the prostitute. They will bring her to ruin and leave her naked; they will eat her flesh and burn her with fire. For God has put it into their hearts to accomplish his purpose" (Rev. 17:16–17).

## The Seventh Bowl—a Severe Earthquake

> The seventh angel poured out his bowl into the air, and out of the temple came a loud voice from the throne, saying, "It is done!" Then there came flashes of lightning, rumblings, peals of thunder and a severe earthquake. No earthquake like it has ever occurred since man has been on earth, so tremendous was the quake. The great city split into three parts, and the cities of the nations collapsed. God remembered Babylon the Great and gave her the cup filled with the wine of the fury of his wrath. Every island fled away and the mountains could not be found. From the sky huge hailstones of about a hundred pounds each fell upon men. And they cursed God on account of the plague of hail, because the plague was so terrible. (Rev. 16:17–21)

## A Holy Slaughter

Underlying forces, hell-bent on destruction, will stir people into delirium. Armageddon will be a war fought with tremendous rage. This holy slaughter will commence with emotions running wild and common sense taking a back seat. Israel's neighboring countries will come to their limit of pain. The masses may believe the great wonders in the sky are a sign from heaven to take back the beloved city. They may also think the plagues are a result of the city's Jewish occupation. Nations will come together and fight to extinguish the Jewish people. In all this madness, the factions at war against Israel will most likely engage in some nuclear exchanges. According to Scripture, blood, fire, and vapors of smoke will fill the battleground.

## The Final Weeks

Jesus included this warning in the Scriptures: "Behold, I come like a thief! Blessed is he who stays awake and keeps his clothes with him, so that he may not go naked and be shamefully exposed" (Rev. 16:15). This warning is penned into Revelation's pages between the sixth and final bowl judgments, which is days away from the Battle of Armageddon and the return of Jesus Christ. This last passage demonstrates that many will not be expecting the return of Jesus Christ when it occurs.

Jesus said men's hearts would fail them for fear of what was lying ahead. This is the hour when the fury of God's wrath is poured out upon mankind, such severe wrath that Christ's church is whisked off the planet! It is written in the Scriptures, "For then there will be great distress, unequaled from the beginning of the world until now—and never to be equaled again" (Matt. 24:21). That's a grim picture. Violent hailstorms, thunder and lightning storms, and raging seas are on the horizon.

Woe to the nations in the Middle East and to the men, women, and children who remain in Jerusalem during Armageddon—that land will become an eerie scene with thick darkness, blood, fire, and death, with the earth shaking and men walking around in a state of delusion.

# The Final Woe

## Armies Surrounding Jerusalem

> When you see Jerusalem being surrounded by armies, you will know that its desolation is near. Then let those who are in Judea flee to the mountains, let those in the city get out, and let those in the country not enter the city. For this is the time of punishment in fulfillment of all that has been written. How dreadful it will be in those days for pregnant women and nursing mothers! There will be great distress in the land and wrath against this people. (Luke 21:20–23)

Armageddon will be a bloodbath. As the armies of Russia, Iran, Libya, and Turkey encompass Israel's border, building up for a strike, it appears, as recorded in Bible prophecy, that the United States, Great Britain, England, Australia, and Canada will protest the action. Nations of Great Britain are spelled out as "Sheba" and "Dedan" in Ezek. 38:13. Most scholars believe that the United States, Australia, and Canada are depicted in the text as "all her villages."

> Sheba and Dedan and the merchants of Tarshish and all her villages will say to you, "Have you come to plunder? Have you gathered your hordes to loot, to carry off silver and gold, to take away livestock and goods and to seize much plunder?" Therefore, son of man, prophesy and say to Gog: "This is what the Sovereign LORD says: In that day, when my people Israel are living in safety, will you not take notice of it? You will come from your place in the far north, you and many nations with you, all of them riding on horses, a great horde, a mighty army. You will advance against my people Israel like a cloud that covers the land. In days to come, O Gog, I will bring you against my land, so that the nations may know me when I show myself holy through you before their eyes." (Ezek. 38:13–16)

Not every nation on the earth will be backing the Antichrist in his attempt to overthrow Jerusalem. The Antichrist's empire will have factions: "He will extend his power over many countries; Egypt will not escape. He will gain control of the treasures of gold and silver and all the riches of Egypt, with the Libyans and Nubians in submission. But reports from the east and the north will alarm him, and he will set out in a great rage to destroy and annihilate many" (Dan. 11:42–44).

The reason Antichrist will never have a strong grip on the entire world is because of the Christians' testimony. People will remember the gospel as they see the events leading to Armageddon unfold.

## Living in Israel a Few Days before Armageddon

A popular world leader who brought peace and safety to the Middle East has just turned the world against the nation of Israel. Like a madman, he has slandered the people, desecrated the Temple, and pronounced himself God. With all the power he can muster, he is gathering his forces in an attempt to destroy Jerusalem and its inhabitants.

Envision what it might be like living in Jerusalem as these events unfold: nature is unloading its fury with the earth quaking, the wind screaming, and terrible signs in the sky! On top of the severe wind, hail, and scorching heat, parts of the city are in ruins and armies are closing in. With bombs exploding near the city's border, the only sensible course of action is to head east for the mountains. As we get out of our cars, we head up into the hills. We sense divine leading. We journey further and see an awesome sight: "On that day his [Jesus'] feet will stand on the Mount of Olives, east of Jerusalem, and the Mount of Olives will be split in two from east to west, forming a great valley, with half of the mountain moving north and half moving south" (Zech. 14:4). Something deep within us is urging us to retreat[125] into this valley. "On that day there will be no light, no cold or frost. It will be a unique day, without daytime or nighttime—a day known to the LORD. When evening comes, there will be light" (Zech. 14:6–7).

At the midnight hour, many from the nation of Israel shall be found huddling in the valley of the Mount of Olives, praying for God's deliverance from imminent destruction. It's from within this valley that the Jewish people learn who their true Messiah is. God will honor their prayers. From this valley of judgment, the Lord shall go forth "like a whirlwind; he will bring down his anger with fury" (Isa. 66:15). Israel will see Jesus coming with the clouds of heaven as the powerful Messiah, mighty to save. They will see the one their fathers pierced, and they will mourn.[126] The eyes of their understanding will be opened. With tears flowing, the Israeli people will be brought back into the fold.[127]

# Chapter 9

# DECEPTION IS ON THE HORIZON

In the final years before Armageddon, earth will behold a manifestation of God flowing through God's people. Through Christ's body jointly connected, Jesus will lead and teach all those who will follow the call. For a while, great revival will sweep through the land, and many will see the light of the Gospel and find the pathway to salvation. Evil men and women will grow to hate the Christians. They will gather together in a rallying cry and denounce the movement. As the underlying forces wage a spiritual battle in the hearts of men, earth's populace will forsake godliness. Wickedness will take over.

As the earth rejects light, it will be given over to gross darkness. Once more, people will choose an evil ruler to rule: they will be given their request. An Antichrist will arise on the world scene with powerful kings backing his empire. Speaking of Antichrist's government, Daniel recorded, "It grew until it reached the host of the heavens, and it threw some of the starry host down to the earth and trampled on them . . . and truth was thrown to the ground" (Dan. 8:10, 12). With truth thrown to the ground, the young, the unpracticed, and the half-committed may lose what truth they once held and accept the devil's lies. Satan will sift the unstable ones among us like wheat. The oil in their lamps will wane, and their lights will flicker and dim.

People strong in Christ, having a solid foundation, will not be shaken in judgment. We know in advance that the seas of trepidation will roar. We know in advance that many of the weak among us will fall. In the wicked days ahead, we will not be tossed and turned, for we have established our house upon the rock of salvation. Let the winds blow. Let the sea roar. Having knowledge of the events to come will make it less difficult for us to stand strong.

Since the beginning of time, every prophet that God has sent into the world to bring deliverance to the people has been put to death by religious people. Once again, the religious throngs will deem God's prophets "worthy of death" (Mark 14:64). We must prepare our hearts and set our faces like flint, walking steadfastly from this evil world into the kingdom of God. Jesus said, "Do not be afraid of what you are about to suffer. I tell you, the devil will put some of you in prison to test you, and you will suffer persecution . . . Be faithful, even to the point of death, and I will give you the crown of life" (Rev. 2:10).

## Seven Years on Earth without Church?

Much of orthodox Christianity is convinced that the church will ascend in the Rapture a full seven years before Armageddon, not just seven weeks, as this book explains. These people interpret the symbolic content of Revelation's chapters in such a manner as to void any application to them; for example, much of the church world is sure that Jesus is the male child in Revelation 12; they believe the woman in the same chapter is Mary. People who see this chapter as a representation of Christ's virgin birth some 2,000 years ago scoff at the idea it may have an application to God's faithful.

Even among the Evangelicals, it is generally taught that the two prophets in Revelation 11 are either John the Baptist and Elijah, or Moses and Elijah and the 144,000 of Revelation 7 are National Israel—they do not see the modern Christian church within this symbolism.[128]

## 2 Thessalonians

The present-day interpretation of the following text is one of the reasons the teaching of a seven-year period on earth void of the church is so widespread. The argument goes like this: where our text reads, "the one who now holds it back," this is said to be all the "Spirit-filled" men, women, and children who make up the church. The text goes on to say, "till he is taken out of the way." This is said to depict the removal of all these Christians—in other words, the Rapture of the church. "For the secret power of lawlessness is already at work; but the one who now holds it back will continue to do so till he is taken out of the way. And then the lawless one will be revealed" (2 Thess. 7–8).

## Sound Teaching Skills—a Small Tangent

While researching doctrine, a teacher should look up every verse pertaining to the subject in question. Upon doing this, one builds a working hypothesis. Some Scriptures at first glance may appear to run contrary to the general theme. Prudent Bible teachers do not use those Scriptures to establish doctrine; they are initially set aside. They first use easier-to-understand proof texts for the foundation until the overall picture comes into view; then after much study, they look into the harder-to-understand verses and bring them into harmony with the general tenor of the main body of evidence. Using this same systematic approach in our study, I have set this Rapture text aside until now: now is the time to bring it into harmony with the general tenor of Scripture:

Several assumptions must be held in order to maintain that this passage in 2 Thessalonians is speaking of the Rapture of the church before the Antichrist reigns. Let's ask ourselves: is there any possibility that Paul was not speaking solely of the church in his discourse? After all, the words *he* and *one* do not demand that the church is the principal subject matter.

Throughout the book of Revelation, we see that God has a restraining force in place to keep Satan in check; we also see this force lifted over and over again as the various events of Revelation transpire. As the Lamb breaks each seal of Revelation's seven-sealed scroll, demon spirits are released to go forth upon Earth. Here is a good example of this force being released: "And the four angels who had been kept ready for this very hour and day and month and year were released to kill a third of mankind" (Rev. 9:15).

The same teachers who maintain that the church is what restrains an event from happening in 2 Thessalonians also claim that the church will have ascended in the Rapture years before the four angels of Rev. 9:15 are released. If there's a force left in place after the church is gone that needs to be lifted before an event can take place on Earth, wouldn't that lessen the possibility that the church is the restraining force in 2 Thessalonians?

Let's continue our investigation by taking a good look at the context of these verses in 2 Thessalonians: "*Concerning the coming of our Lord Jesus Christ and our being gathered to him, we ask you, brothers, not to become easily unsettled or alarmed by some prophecy, report or letter supposed to have come from us, saying that the day of the Lord has already come. Don't let anyone deceive you in any way, for that day will not come until the rebellion occurs and the man of lawlessness is revealed, the man doomed to destruction*" (2 Thess. 2:1–3).

There is strong reason to believe that this warning from Paul starts off speaking about the First Resurrection with the words "Concerning the coming of our Lord Jesus Christ and our being gathered to him." Then Paul shifts his focus to an event that is called "the day of the Lord." When discussing Bible prophecy, the terms *day of the Lord* and *Rapture/Resurrection* are not randomly interchanged. *The day of the Lord* speaks of Christ's Millennial Kingdom, starting with God's wrath upon earth, while the *First Resurrection* precedes God's wrath. The final factor that must be accepted in order to maintain this position is that when Paul speaks of "that day" in verse 3, he is speaking of the Rapture from verse 1 and not the day of the Lord from verse 2. If Paul were speaking of the day of the Lord in our text when he penned "that day," this teaching would fail.

## The Day of the Lord in Scripture

1. "Woe to you who long for the day of the LORD! Why do you long for the day of the LORD? That day will be darkness, not light. It will be as though a man fled from a lion only to meet a bear" (Amos 5:18–19).
2. "A day of the LORD is coming when your plunder will be divided among you. I will gather all the nations to Jerusalem to fight against it; the city will be captured, the houses ransacked, and the women raped" (Zech. 14:1–2).
3. "The great day of the LORD is near—near and coming quickly. Listen! The cry on the day of the LORD will be bitter, the shouting of the warrior there. That day will be a day of wrath, a day of distress and anguish, a day of trouble and ruin, a day of darkness and gloom, a day of clouds and blackness" (Zeph. 14–15).
4. "The day of the LORD is great; it is dreadful. Who can endure it? . . . The sun will be turned to darkness and the moon to blood before the coming of the great and dreadful day of the LORD" (Joel 2:11, 31).

The *day of the Lord* speaks of a time when the nations are punished. This day also encompasses Christ's return and the duration of His kingdom. If this is what Paul is referring to in 2 Thessalonians when he penned, "Don't let anyone deceive you in any way, for that day will not come until the rebellion occurs and the man of lawlessness is revealed," then Paul was no longer speaking of the Rapture—Paul had moved on and was speaking of Christ's kingdom.

During Paul's day, there was a widespread teaching[129] that maintained the world had entered into the millennial kingdom. Paul was addressing the church, defending against this teaching by expressing that there was yet to come "the coming of our Lord Jesus Christ and our being gathered to him." To strengthen his position, Paul went on to explain that there was another event that must also occur before *the day of the Lord*, which is the revealing of the "man of lawlessness."

In order for this verse in 2 Thessalonians to make sense, we need to admit that Paul was speaking of two events in his discourse, and once we have done this, this Scripture no longer offers proof that the church will be caught up as soon as the Antichrist is revealed. Understanding that Paul was not expressing that the church would be caught up before the Antichrist reigns brings the understanding of this verse into harmony with the rest of the Bible.

## Christians—Still on Earth

"And I saw the souls of those who had been beheaded because of their testimony for Jesus and because of the word of God. They had not worshiped the beast or his image and had not received his mark on their foreheads or their hands" (Rev. 20:4). Because it is said of them, they "had not received his mark on their foreheads," this demonstrates that these people were still on the earth during Antichrist's reign. The following verse says that they are a part of the "first resurrection." Two resurrections are spoken of in Scripture: in the first one, the dead will be raised and those "who are still alive and are left will be caught up together with them in the clouds to meet the Lord in the air" (1 Thess. 4:17). The second resurrection takes place a thousand years later. So these people not only lived on earth under Antichrist, but they took part in the Rapture as well.

"And I saw what looked like a sea of glass mixed with fire and, standing beside the sea, those who had been victorious over the beast and his image and over the number of his name" (Rev. 15:2–3). This verse also shows Christians who had been living on earth during the Antichrist's system; these souls are now seen in heaven right before the bowls of wrath are poured out. Could this verse demonstrate that they, too, have ascended in the Rapture?

"As I watched, this horn was waging war against the saints and defeating them . . . He will speak against the Most High and oppress his saints and try to change the set times and the laws. The saints will be handed over to him for a time, times and half a time" (Dan. 7:21, 25). This "horn" is Antichrist. The "saints" are all the Christians who make up the church. This word usage in Daniel, "time, times and half a time" and the identical word usage in Rev. 12:12, "time, times and half a time," are speaking of a three-and-a-half-year period in which the Antichrist rules the world. Our text goes on to say, "Then the dragon was enraged at the woman and went off to make war against the rest of her offspring—those who obey God's commandments and hold to the testimony of Jesus" (Rev. 12:17). The woman is the church: her offspring is also a part of the church. Could this last text speak any clearer of Christian persecution during the time of Antichrist's government?

The teaching that Christians will have ascended before Antichrist reigns, as found in the current interpretation of our 2 Thessalonians text, runs contrary to all these Bible verses, whose interpretations are straightforward. It also goes against the teaching of a last trumpet Rapture and violates the whole design of Revelation. The earth will not be void of the church a full seven years before Armageddon. The two witnesses are seen performing miracle-working power as they deliver their testimony, and if the witnesses are an illustration of the church, then surely the church is still on the earth as Revelation's days unfold.

Jesus said, "But understand this: If the owner of the house had known at what time of night the thief was coming, he would have kept watch and would not have let his house be broken into. So you also must be ready, because the Son of Man will come at an hour when you do not expect him" (Matt. 24:43–44). With so many awaiting Christ's return, it seems unusual that he could appear when we aren't looking—unless our teachers have misled us by maintaining theories about his return that are in error? It's recorded in Scripture that when many are sure the prophecies concerning Christ's return have failed, "they will say, 'Where is this "coming" he promised?'" (2 Pet. 3:4). For them, "the day of the Lord will come like a thief" (2 Pet. 3:10).

## In the Days of the Seventh Trumpet

One of the great truths this work established is that the Rapture occurs in the days of the seventh trumpet when it shall begin to sound. It happens right before the bowl plagues are poured out. This understanding has changed the way many of us look at Revelation. Instead of seven years on earth void of the church, Revelation's pages speak of men, women, and children delivering a testimony to the world!

As Jesus breaks open the first wax seal of earth's mortgage scroll in heaven, a countdown begins. No one knows this day or hour. Nevertheless, we understand from Scripture that the breaking of the first seal signifies that earth's domain is about to be transferred.

## In the Middle of the Final Week—the Messiah Was Cut Off

It only makes sense that something is standing in the way of Christ's kingdom: otherwise, why would God have allowed Satan to continue ruling the earth for the last two thousand years? According to

Old Testament prophecy, Christ's ministry was cut off in the middle[130] of the week of years that was needed to fulfill the covenant. With all the pain and suffering in the world, if it was lawful for Jesus to step in and put a stop to the suffering, it would seem likely that he would have by now. There's a reason Christ isn't ruling the earth at this time! He's waiting for the final three and a half years of legal testimony to be delivered through His spiritual body: "This is a profound mystery—but I am talking about Christ and the church" (Eph. 5:32).

## Three and One-Half Years

Within the Book of Revelation there are several places where a period of three and a half years is recorded:

1. "The beast was given a mouth to utter proud words and blasphemies and to exercise his authority for forty-two months" (Rev. 13:5).
2. "The woman was given the two wings of a great eagle, so that she might fly to the place prepared for her in the desert, where she would be taken care of for a time, times and half a time, out of the serpent's reach" (Rev. 12:14).
3. "But after the three and a half days a breath of life from God entered them, and they stood on their feet, and terror struck those who saw them" (Rev. 11:11).

"Forty-two months," "three and a half days," "time, times and half a time," and "1,260 days," are all terms depicting a three-and-a-half-year time frame. Some people put two of these periods back to back and get a seven-year time frame. This is a possible interpretation, because in Revelation 11, it's recorded that the two witnesses prophesy for 1,260 days, and then they are killed and their bodies lie in the street for three and a half days. The term three and a half days in our text is probably speaking of the three-and-a-half-year period that Antichrist reigns.

However, let's use common sense here: within Revelation's chapters, events overlap; sometimes an event is mentioned, and then the reader is brought back in time to focus on elements of that event from a different perspective. Everything in chapter 11 is not as cut and dried as it appears. The time frame represents events that are impossible to put in a finite framework.

## Stealing the Calling

Perhaps Satan's greatest triumph lies in stealing the calling that we have found in God's Word. Satan knows he can't remove us from the Master's hand, so instead he focuses on sidetracking us to forsake the Master's plan. Satan works within and without the church, desperately seeking to corrupt the gospel. He's the source of bitter waters—corrupt teachings that lead men astray. The pure water of the Word cleanses the soul. Righteous teaching brings forth good fruit and a bountiful harvest. But when the church receives false teaching, it's a detriment to the body. At this very hour, Satan is lashing out in an attempt to hinder the growing kingdom of Christ where it matters the most—by influencing us to abandon the Great Commission. If the devil can stop the mouths of the prophets, he can choke the wellspring of life from the movement.

Deception is on the horizon! Souls are hanging in the balance. Millions are standing on the brink of eternity. Satan and his angels are pushing hard, focusing all their effort on deceiving the minds of men and then keeping them in deception. Satan desires to condemn as many as possible to the same fate he's facing by influencing them to believe things that will lead to their spiritual destruction. Without the light of truth, it will be impossible for some to see through the coming darkness.

## Christ Is Calling Us to Warn the World

The most consequential theme Revelation holds is that we, as a unified body, have a ministry to fulfill in these last days. Keeping this vision fresh in our hearts will keep us open to the moving of God's Spirit. The Spirit will lead us. The Spirit will teach us. The Spirit will give us words to speak as we bring forth our testimony. Jesus said, "And this gospel of the kingdom will be preached in the whole world as a testimony to all nations, and then the end will come" (Matt. 24:14).

# Chapter 10

# THE OVERCOMING CHURCH IN PROPHECY

Many of the groups within Revelation's pages are composed of people that had once died. These assemblies, such as "the twenty-four elders,"[131] "the great multitude,"[132] the "souls"[133] under the altar and the "Lamb"[134] are illustrations of the church in heaven with Jesus Christ standing as head. Much of the events that occur in the book of Revelation are the direct result of prayers[135] from these various groups. The woman as found in Revelation's 12th chapter is an illustration of the Heavenly church and the male child she brings forth represents Jesus Christ along with a ruling class that gains access to the throne.

It's written of this child, "She gave birth to a son, a male child, who will rule all the nations with an iron scepter" (Rev. 12:5). On this subject Jesus proclaimed,

> To him who overcomes and does my will to the end, I will give authority over the nations—'He will rule them with an iron scepter; he will dash them to pieces like pottery— just as I have received authority from my Father.' (Rev. 2:26)

As Christ and his church take authority in heaven Satan is banished to the earth; then a loud voice in heaven says, "Now have come the salvation and the power and the kingdom of our God, and the authority of his Christ. For the accuser of our brothers, who accuses them before our God day and night, has been hurled down" (Rev 12:10).

As Satan is no longer able to approach the heavenly throne waging accusations at the church in heaven, he initiates an all out war with the church on earth. As it is written, "Then the dragon was enraged at the woman and went off to make war against the rest of her offspring—those who obey God's commandments and hold to the testimony of Jesus" (Rev. 12:17).

There are parallels between the woman and her offspring from Revelation 12 and the woman and her offspring from Genesis and Isaiah. These are fascinating prophecies because they go into details about the role of the church in the last days.

## The Woman and Her Offspring from Genesis

Because of the fall of man and the role Satan played in man's fall back in the Garden of Eden, God spoke these words to the serpent, "I will put enmity between you and the woman, and between your offspring and hers; he will crush your head, and you will strike his heel" (Gen. 3:15).

Many teachers believe the offspring from the woman in this prophecy is Jesus Christ, and that analogy does apply. The first woman Eve is the Mother of us all, including Christ. Jesus certainly did "crush" the head of the serpent (Satan) figuratively speaking when he atoned for the sins of mankind upon the cross. Satan no longer "holds the power of death"[136] over us because of Christ's sacrifice. Yet, there is more to the woman's offspring than the physical lineage of Jesus, and there is more to this illustration of the woman's seed crushing the serpent's head and the serpent striking his heel than the struggle between Christ and Satan 2,000 years ago. This prophecy has a spiritual fulfillment with Jesus Christ and his collective body (the church) interacting with Satan and his entourage at the end of time.

In the original Hebrew language in which Genesis was written, the word "crush" is showing us a deathblow to the head. In all of Scripture, the only place there is a serpent mentioned that has received a death wound to the head by the seed of a woman is in the book of Revelation 13:3. Revelation 13 is mostly about Antichrist's rise to power and the persecution of God's people. Therefore, way down at the end of time we will see the fulfillment to this prophecy from Genesis. Satan will be banished from the presence of God's throne, never to be allowed access to the heavens again. This banishment from heaven has much to do with crushing the head of the serpent, however the church on earth may also play a significant role in dealing the deathblow.

## The First Woman with Child from Isaiah

> As a woman with child and about to give birth writhes and cries out in her pain, so were we in your presence, O LORD. We were with child, we writhed in pain, but we gave birth to wind. We have not brought salvation to the earth; we have not given birth to people of the world. (Isa. 26:17-18)

It's obvious that this is not "a woman" in a natural sense. The word "we" is found in the passage six times. The word usage itself suggests a figurative interpretation: "so were we in your presence". "We were with child." "We writhed in pain." "We gave birth to wind." "We have not brought salvation to the earth." "We have not given birth to people of the world." The "we" in this prophecy is a reference to God's people. God's people are shown going through the pains of labor, figurative speaking, with the anticipated result of bringing salvation to the earth.

This prophecy gives the impression that the church is suffering as a woman in labor. She is in pain trying to bring forth offspring. The context of this passage is in the last days right before the first resurrection/rapture as shown by the following verse: "But your dead will live; their bodies will rise. You who dwell in the dust, wake up and shout for joy. Your dew is like the dew of the morning; the earth will give birth to her dead" (Isa. 26:19).

God is assuring the church consisting of both the dead and the living that she will have a fruitful offspring regardless of how bleak things look in the natural. Could this end-time prophecy be showing us a church struggling to fulfill Christ's great commission?

## The Second Woman with Child from Isaiah

> "Before she goes into labor, she gives birth; before the pains come upon her, she delivers a son. Who has ever heard of such a thing? Who has ever seen such things? Can a country be born in a day or a nation be brought forth in a moment? Yet no sooner is Zion in labor than she gives birth to her children. Do I bring to the moment of birth and not give delivery?' says the LORD. 'Do I close up the womb when I bring to delivery?' says your God. 'Rejoice with Jerusalem and be glad for her, all you who love her; rejoice greatly with her, all you who mourn over her. For you will nurse and be satisfied at her comforting breasts; you will drink deeply and delight in her overflowing abundance". (Isa. 66:7-11)

Let's go through this prophecy verse by verse:
Isaiah 66:

Verse 7.
"Before she goes into labor, she gives birth; before the pains come upon her, she delivers a son."

This verse is expressing something that is impossible in the natural because no woman on earth can give birth before she goes into labor. This saying has to do with time: "Before" is the key word here, it is used twice in our text. Let's ask the question what son did the church deliver "before" it entered into labor? The answer is Jesus Christ.

> Verse 8.
> "Who has ever heard of such a thing? Who has ever seen such things? Can a country be born in a day or a nation be brought forth in a moment? Yet no sooner is Zion in labor than she gives birth to her children."

In this verse we have a contrast between a single "thing" the birth of Christ, and plural "things" the birth of children. The words "a nation" speaks of a great multitude of people. We also notice the words "no sooner;" this appears to imply that as the church first enters labor offspring are produced. Labor implies a spiritual struggle. Since this labor is an illustration of a spiritual event we can assume that the birth is also of a spiritual nature. On this subject Jesus said, "Flesh gives birth to flesh, but the Spirit gives birth to spirit. You should not be surprised at my saying, 'You must be born again.' The wind blows wherever it pleases. You hear its sound, but you cannot tell where it comes from or where it is going. So it is with everyone born of the Spirit" (John 3:6-8).

This saying, "Yet no sooner is Zion in labor than she gives birth to her children" implies that as the church first encounters a struggle in the spirit, most likely from satanic persecution, multitudes of people will come into the Christian faith.

> Verse 9.
> "'Do I bring to the moment of birth and not give delivery?' says the LORD. 'Do I close up the womb when I bring to delivery?' says your God."

God is promising us that no matter how impossible things look in the natural this spiritual "birth" will take place. God is also saying that He is the author of this thing and He will finish what He starts. This fruitful multiplication of God's faithful will be accomplished through a work in God's Spirit as it is written: "I" will bring to delivery.

> Verse 10-11
> "Rejoice with Jerusalem and be glad for her, all you who love her; rejoice greatly with her, all you who mourn over her. For you will nurse and be satisfied at her comforting breasts; you will drink deeply and delight in her overflowing abundance."

Zion and Jerusalem are illustrations of God's covenant people; in the New Testament this would mean the church. It's the church that will give "birth to her children" and "nurse" her young. This prophecy in Isaiah had its initial fulfillment in the days when Christ walked the earth and shortly thereafter when the church was first born. A nation was "born in a day". Many people were nursed, figuratively speaking, from the teachings of Christ and the Apostolic church. Yet, the devil was quick to bring persecution upon the Christian movement from powerful emperors and corrupt religious rulers.

## History Will Repeat Itself

The next fulfillment of this prophecy will be in the days ahead, shortly before and during the time of Antichrist's regime. History is bound to repeat itself. A great light will sweep over the land much like it did in the days of the early church, then just like in times past the world will plunge into darkness. Through the administration of a powerful emperor and a false religious system[137] the developing Christian movement will be overthrown.

Now when they have finished their testimony, the beast that comes up from the Abyss will attack them, and overpower and kill them. (Rev 11:7)

## War and Victory

There's no doubt that Christians will be martyred in the days ahead as recorded in our last text. In the natural, by all human observations, it may appear that Satan will bring humanity into complete subjection. The Antichrist will receive deification from the masses. By his administration Satan will stir humanity into a killing frenzy. Every logical reason will be given to wipe Christians from off the face of the planet. The devil is seen coming to the earth with the intent of waging war and a satanic war is exactly what we shall face. In any war there are bound to be casualties. Innocent blood will be shed. However, war also has an upside. We shall be victorious.

## The End-time Church

The church has a ministry to perform in the last days, that ministry is to bring salvation to the earth. Jesus said, "And this gospel of the kingdom will be preached in the whole world as a testimony to all nations, and then the end will come" (Matt. 24:14).

The bulk of Revelation 11 is an illustration of the end-time church. Although the description of her ministry is penned in highly figurative language the point being made is clear: the word of God will go forth with great power. Then in Revelation 12 we see the church again, she is illustrated as a woman with offspring, and once more she is seen bringing forth a testimony. "They overcame him by the blood of the Lamb and by the word of their testimony…" (Rev 12:11). What we see throughout Revelation is a victorious church. We see a church that is turning the world upside down for Jesus Christ. A church composed of believers that will not back down to the edicts of Satan. A church that stands strong and fights the good fight of faith, and when the battle is over reigns with Christ in the Promised Land.

> I saw thrones on which were seated those who had been given authority to judge. And I saw the souls of those who had been beheaded because of their testimony for Jesus and because of the word of God. They had not worshiped the beast or his image and had not received his mark on their foreheads or their hands. They came to life and reigned with Christ a thousand years. (Rev. 20:4)

# Chapter 11

# CHOOSE YOUR BATTLES CAREFULLY

An enemy is coming to our shore. A vicious, bitter attack will soon be launched. Mankind will be subjected to the edicts of a detestable being whose goal is to enslave, injure and kill. This monster will not be satisfied with only forcing his opponents to die. His plan is to bring death[138] to even his most devoted followers.

Rebellion[139] is the cause of the coming conflict. Vengeance[140] will be the motive behind the slaughter. Deception[141] is the means by which the battle will be fought. Even now the stage is being set for the war. One day we'll have to choose sides. Will we submit to the adversary when he comes to our homeland? Will we bow down and worship his image? Will we follow his edicts? When the greatest terrorist who has ever lived endeavors to take away our freedom; will we surrender our will to him, or will we fight?

## John's Vision of the Beast

The Apostle John had a vision of the future and saw Satan being cast out of heaven to the earth. He then saw a beast emerge from the sea and have an impact upon humanity. All of the things that John saw were illustrations of real events that will take place in the days ahead.

Let's look at John's vision:
Revelation 13

Verse 1.
And I saw a beast coming out of the sea. He had ten horns and seven heads, with ten crowns on his horns, and on each head a blasphemous name.

Earlier in Revelation before Satan was banished from heaven he was illustrated as "an enormous red dragon with seven heads and ten horns and seven crowns on his heads."[142] In John's next view of the beast where he is seen coming out of the sea three crowns have been added to his horns. Three added crowns are indications that the satanic empire has now grown stronger.

The sea the beast arises from is an illustration of the "nations;" this is spelled out in Revelation[143] as well as in Daniel.[144] The Scriptures also tell us what the ten horns represent; "'The ten horns you saw are ten kings who have not yet received a kingdom, but who for one hour will receive authority as kings along with the beast'" (Rev. 17:12).

A popular theory about the ten kings is that they represent the European Common Market. One drawback to the theory is that the Bible claims they are "ten kings who have not yet received a kingdom". However, the European Common Market is made up of existing kingdoms. While some Bible teachers harmonize this potential discrepancy others believe that Revelation's ten kings could be powerful men and women that are now behind the scenes and "who for one hour will receive authority as kings along with the beast."

The crowns most likely speak of the authority that a king possesses. The blasphemous names written upon each head clearly indicates that every branch of this beast/government is in total rebellion against God.

## Three Plus Four Equals Seven

The prophet Daniel also had a vision of a ten-horned beast. It was the last of the four beasts that Daniel saw rising out of a great sea. An angel explained to Daniel that, "'The four great beasts are four kingdoms that will rise from the earth.'" The first beast in Daniel's vision was "like a lion."[145] The second beast was "like a bear."[146] The third beast "looked like a leopard"[147] and the fourth beast that Daniel saw was "frightening and very powerful. It had large iron teeth; it crushed and devoured its victims and trampled underfoot whatever was left. It was different from all the former beasts, and it had ten horns" (Dan. 7:7).

From the time Daniel received his vision to the return of Jesus Christ the world will have seen four more beast/empires. This fourth beast is the same as the seven-headed, ten-horned beast, in Revelation. Since the beginning of creation there have been six world empires: Egypt, Assyria, Babylon, Media-Persia, Greece, and Rome. The next one would make seven; hence the seven-headed beast to come.

The Book of Revelation explains it this way: the seven heads are "seven kings. Five have fallen, one is, the other has not yet come; but when he does come, he must remain for a little while" (Rev. 17:10). The five kingdoms that had fallen at the time Revelation was penned were Egypt, Assyria, Babylon, Media-Persia and Greece. Rome was a world empire then and so it was written of Rome, "one is."

# World Empires—Then And Now
## Revelation 13 Continued

Verse 2.
The beast I saw resembled a leopard, but had feet like those of a bear and a mouth like that of a lion. The dragon gave the beast his power and his throne and great authority.

This beast appears to have attributes from every former monarchy yet the scriptures clearly state that it will be different. Possibly the reason this last monarchy will be different is because none of the previous kingdoms had command over large areas of the earth. The technology to communicate between generals and officers in real time across land and sea was nonexistent in times past. Now along with global telecommunications, the modern war machine is capable of lambasting opposing forces on a scale never before seen in human history. The superior military power the modern emperor will have at his disposal is surely one of the qualities that will make the New World Order much different that any former kingdom.

Also, in the area of economic sanctions, the New World Order will have far-reaching control over its subjects. No former empire the world has ever seen has had the ability to force everyone "to receive a mark on his right hand or on his forehead, so that no one could buy or sell unless he had the mark" (Rev. 13:16-17).

Finally, in the area of religion, the new monarchy will exceed every former one. A new-age counterfeit church will go hand in hand with Satan's Order. The "false prophet"[148] will work alongside the Antichrist and perform "great and miraculous signs"[149] deceiving the nations with his satanic "power."[150] In Revelation 17 this religious system is pictured as a woman sitting upon a seven headed ten-horned beast. She is called "the great prostitute, who sits on many waters"[151] which is an illustration of a harlot church with global participation. Revelation speaks of her as having committed "adulteries"[152] meaning that she has seduced her congregation into a relationship with Satan rather than the true husband[153] of the church—the LORD Almighty. The Apostle John "saw that the woman was drunk with the blood of the saints, the blood of those who bore testimony to Jesus" (Rev. 17:6). This is a good description of the multitudes[154] of Christians who will be martyred because of persecution from the coming satanic religion.

## The Beast's Fatal Wound
Revelation 13 continued

> Verse 3.
> One of the heads of the beast seemed to have had a fatal wound, but the fatal wound had been healed. The whole world was astonished and followed the beast.

It's interesting to note that before Antichrist appears upon the world scene this satanic beast/empire is pictured as having a fatal wound. Could the light[155] of the gospel shining upon Satan's dark[156] kingdom be the fatal blow that wounds the empire in its initial stages?

Imagine what it will be like in the days ahead as millions of Bible believing Christians see prophecy coming to pass. Those among us who are strong in the faith will desire to become "witnesses"[157] for Christ and help to fulfill his Great Commission; bringing the gospel to the ends of the earth.

For a while, revival will sweep over the land. In the last days the Christian church will grow in record numbers, but there will come a time when the faith of the newborn will be put to the test. Satan will come at the church as a roaring lion. He will prey upon the weak. The partially committed will suffer the most. Banished from heaven and knowing full well that he has only a short time left to deceive the nations Satan will redouble his efforts. As the devil and his host bring in a new monarchy that's only purpose is to eradicate Christianity some of us will stand strong, yet many shall fall.

## Satan Worship
Revelation 13 Continued

Verse 4.
Men worshiped the dragon because he had given authority to the beast, and they also worshiped the beast and asked, "Who is like the beast? Who can make war against him?"

Satan will be praised for establishing this kingdom upon the earth. Many will welcome the New World Order as an essential component of a utopian society. The government to come will have lots of appeal. It will be the answer to man's problems. It will provide economic stability and trade through a network of financial institutions. It will bring about world peace through a unified coalition of nations. It will provide a sense of safety from the threat of war and terrorism. The words, "'Who is like the beast? Who can make war against him?'" speaks of great military capability. Enormous military strength along with the control of every person's monetary transactions will make this a formidable beast indeed.

## The Mouth of the Beast
Revelation 13 Continued

Verse 5.
The beast was given a mouth to utter proud words and blasphemies and to exercise his authority for forty-two months.

Here, where we see "the beast was given a mouth" this passage is speaking of the man Antichrist. "He opened his mouth to blaspheme God, and to slander his name and his dwelling place and those who live in heaven. He was given power to make war against the saints and to conquer them. And he was given authority over every tribe, people, language and nation" (Rev. 13:6-7).

The word "saints" in this passage is speaking of Christians. Satan is going to give his power to the Antichrist in an attempt to conquer the Christians and dominate the rest of humanity. The word conquer can mean, defeat, overpower, beat, or triumph over. The whole idea behind the word conquer is to "obtain by force."

## Portrait of an Antichrist

> In the latter part of their reign, when rebels have become completely wicked, a stern-faced king, a master of intrigue, will arise. He will become very strong, but not by his own power. He will cause astounding devastation and will succeed in whatever he does. (Dan. 8:23-24)

A powerful figure will arise upon the world scene. He will consider himself superior[158] to all men. The kingdoms of the world will be delivered into his hand. He will not honor the God of his fathers, "nor will he regard any god, but will exalt himself above all that is worshiped."[159] Rising up from among his peers this wicked one will sell his soul to do Satan's bidding. "Lucifer"[160] who deceived a host of angels and plunged humanity into the darkness of sin will take on human form. The devil will manifest himself through his christ and walk and talk among the children of men. He will have "the eyes of a man and a mouth that will speak boastfully."[161]

> He will speak against the Most High and oppress his saints and try to change the set times and the laws. The saints will be handed over to him for a time, times and half a time. (Dan. 7:25)

It's interesting to note that Antichrist will openly speak out against God. The world will hear the ideologies of the devil right from the source. Satan shall spit forth his twisted delusions through his mouthpiece. He will be given three and one half years to rule and during this time Christians will face severe persecution.

One might wonder why God will allow the devil and all of the fallen angels to dominate mankind with such power in the days to come? The answer is simple: at this point in time a great light will have come into the world through Christians spreading the gospel. As the world rejects the light of Christ, God will allow great darkness to cover the land. Because people will have rejected the truth they will be given over to a reprobate mind. In a state of madness the deceived[162] masses will persecute those who have witnessed to them about Jesus and will celebrate[163] the killing of God's prophets.

## A Thousand Points of Darkness

The devil has had thousands of years to refine his approach to man. He has seen what methods have brought results and he has witnessed what tactics have failed. From the very beginning Satan understood that he needed to keep the light of truth from shining on his prey. If people could see that it was really Satan who was goading them to take certain pathways in life, they would never walk down those paths. Satan through the Antichrist shall deceive the nations. The devil will endeavor to bring the whole world into rebellion against God.

In a vain attempt to forgo the inevitable[164] Satan and his demon host will fight down to the last hour. As the final curtain of human history is drawing to a close the devil will look across the vast sea of humanity that he had duped into following him in his own failed coup against the Almighty. What will he see in their faces? Will he see men and women who were proud that they gave their eternal lives to bolster his image? Or will his followers mock him in derision when they finally see things clearly? The Bible paints a picture of the devil as he awaits his judgment, it portrays his followers marveling over him saying, "Is this the one who shook the earth and made kingdoms tremble, the one who made the world a desolate place, who overthrew its cities…?"[165]

Satan will go down in history as having conceived and carried out the worst plan ever! Instead of staying within the Creator's graces and enjoying an eternal paradise in God's presence, Satan along with all of his followers will have hell to pay. The words to the song "I did it my way" will have no redeeming value on judgment day. On that day many tormented souls will be lamenting over their rebellious attitudes. Undoubtedly throngs of human souls standing before the judgment seat will be thinking about the decisions they made that put them at odds with God, wishing beyond hope that they had yielded to the truth of the gospel that could have saved them.

## Marching to the Front Lines

What can we do to help the masses? As warriors in God's army we can do much more than merely hold our ground. The best defense is a strong offence. When the enemy is holding nothing back in his onslaught against humanity why should we merely shield ourselves from his blows. In order to be effective soldiers we need to march ahead to the front lines where we can strike back. Instead of hiding in our prayer closets let's take the gospel of Jesus Christ to the streets. Let's reach out to the children in darkness and show them the light. People that are brought out from the grip of

Satan will be forever grateful to the ones that cared enough to free them.

> Those who are wise will shine like the brightness of the heavens, and those who lead many to righteousness, like the stars for ever and ever. (Dan. 12:3)

Chapter  12

# PARADISE RESTORED

In the beginning of this book, we envisioned Paradise. Adam and Eve were living in the Garden of Eden. There were no bugs to bite them, no thorns to hurt them, and the curse man now suffers was not in effect. Eden was the most beautiful place on the face of the planet. Every tree was pleasant to behold. There was an abundance of water. God had put it in the hearts of the animals to revere man. Nothing was to be hurt in God's holy mountain. Death had yet to leave its stain. The Lord God was walking in the garden in the cool of the day, fellowshipping with His children. This natural earthly scene represents the future paradise God has for us in heaven. However, before we all go over yonder, the kingdom Christ spoke of [166] must first come to earth. Once again this earth will blossom.[167] "No longer will there be any curse."[168]

At this time, earth is a far cry from the serene planet it once was—wickedness, corruption, sin, and death now reign. Therefore God will bring the earth back into its former glory.

"Never again will there be in it an infant who lives but a few days, or an old man who does not live out his years; he who dies at a hundred will be thought a mere youth; he who fails to reach a hundred will be considered accursed. They will build houses and dwell in them; they will plant vineyards and eat their fruit. No longer will they build houses and others live in them, or plant and others eat. For as the days of a tree, so will be the days of my people; my chosen ones will long enjoy the works of their hands. They will not toil in vain or bear children doomed to misfortune; for they will be a people blessed by the Lord, they and their descendants with them. Before they call I will answer; while they are still speaking I will hear. The wolf and the lamb will feed together, and the lion will eat straw like the ox, but dust will be the serpent's food. They will neither harm nor destroy on all my holy mountain," says the Lord. (Isa. 65:20–25)

This passage squarely depicts life on earth during Christ's kingdom. And here's why:

1. Isaiah speaks of "he who dies." Yet Jesus said, "In the resurrection from the dead . . . they can no longer die; for they are like the angels" (Luke 20:35–36). So this passage must be referring to a time before the general resurrection.
2. In Isaiah it's written, "He who fails to reach a hundred will be considered accursed." This is another reference to death. It's also pointing to the truth that people should expect to see a limited, yet lengthy life.
3. Isaiah speaks of people building houses, planting vineyards, and living as long as a tree. Before the flood, man's average life span was between 830 to 912 years.[169]
4. Isaiah speaks of people bearing children and having descendants.
5. One significant factor is that the lion will eat straw like the ox. In Eden, Adam and Eve were vegetarians.

6. The final point is that dust will be the serpent's food. This has figurative meaning because a reptile cannot live on dust. Could this be in reference to Satan's absence as he is banished from the earth for Christ's thousand-year reign?

"The infant will play near the hole of the cobra, and the young child put his hand into the viper's nest" (Isa. 11:8). Even formerly venomous snakes will pose no threat in Paradise.

# A Thousand Years

> He seized the dragon, that ancient serpent, who is the devil, or Satan, and bound him for a thousand years. He threw him into the Abyss, and locked and sealed it over him, to keep him from deceiving the nations anymore until the thousand years were ended. After that, he must be set free for a short time. And I saw the souls of those who had been beheaded because of their testimony for Jesus and because of the word of God. They had not worshiped the beast or his image and had not received his mark on their foreheads or their hands. They came to life and reigned with Christ a thousand years. (Rev. 20:2–4)

God will remove Satan from his position as earth's ruler and shut him up in a prison. The dominance of the earth will then[170] be given over to Christ. The Christians who took part in the first resurrection, the resurrection that comes a thousand years earlier than the general resurrection, will also take part in this kingdom. We shall have glorified bodies, and Jesus will appoint us positions[171] in his government. All of the people who had lived and died during the thousand years, along with all those who were not a part of Christ's millennial reign, will be raised at the end of the thousand years. Concerning this resurrection, Jesus said: "Do not be amazed at this, for a time is coming when all who are in their graves will hear his voice and come out—those who have done good will rise to live, and those who have done evil will rise to be condemned" (John 5:28–29).

## Christ's Kingdom

The whole world will see Christ's majesty as he sets forth to bring in a kingdom of righteousness. "Come, let us return to the Lord. He has torn us to pieces but he will heal us; he has injured us but he will bind up our wounds. After two days he will revive us; on the third day he will restore us, that we may live in his presence" (Hos. 6:1–2). Could these days in Hosea represent thousand-year periods? It's been almost two thousand years since Jerusalem was burned and God's covenant people were driven out of the Holy City.

## Prophetic Symbolism

As we look into a few Old Testament passages that depict the coming kingdom of Christ, let's understand how to interpret the prophetic symbolism in the light of common sense and sound scriptural principles. "At that time they will call Jerusalem the throne of the Lord, and all nations will gather in Jerusalem to honor the name of the Lord. No longer will they follow the stubbornness of their evil hearts" (Jer. 3:17). There are many Scriptures pointing to Jerusalem as being the place where Christ will set up his kingdom; however, this city in Bible prophecy transcends finite boundaries, for Jerusalem in prophecy is a symbolic illustration of the perfected church.

> In the last days the mountain of the Lord's temple will be established as chief among the mountains; it will be raised above the hills, and all nations will stream to it. Many peoples will come and say, "Come, let us go up to the mountain of the Lord, to the house of the God of Jacob. He will teach us his ways, so that we may walk in his paths." (Isa. 2:2–3)

Terms like "chief among the mountains" and "above the hills" demonstrate that this passage is a prophetic illustration. This verse is crying out a spiritual truth. The Lord's house will be the highest position on earth indeed, yet not in a literal sense. The Lord's house will be upon the highest mountain symbolically. Jesus will hold the highest office in the earth, standing as King of Kings. Christ's position will overshadow every former world government. And Christ will reign from Jerusalem, spiritually speaking. Let's ask the question: where does Jesus reign right now? The answer is, in the hearts of his children.

## The Pull from Satan

The devil will be chained for Christ's thousand-year reign; therefore, the pull from Satan to tempt men and hinder man's spiritual development will not be a factor to stunt man's growth. Everything that exalts itself against the knowledge of God will be cast down. The glory of Jesus will be lifted high. Men and women, through yielding to the spirit of Christ and feeding upon the Word of God, will set out on a journey to spiritual perfection. Every thought will be brought into obedience of Christ.

This next passage illustrates the new earth after this one has been dissolved. It depicts eternity, yet also has an application in the Millennium.

## The New Jerusalem

> Then I saw a new heaven and a new earth, for the first heaven and the first earth had passed away, and there was no longer any sea. I saw the Holy City, the new Jerusalem, coming down out of heaven from God, prepared as a bride beautifully dressed for her husband. And I heard a loud voice from the throne saying, "Now the dwelling of God is with men, and he will live with them. They will be his people, and God himself will be with them and be their God." (Rev. 21:1–3)

This "new Jerusalem" is an illustration depicting the church. This city of Jerusalem returns from heaven with Christ at the beginning of the millennium. It is from within this city that Jesus will rule. From this city, the Word of the Lord will come into the earth: the glory of Christ will go forth from Jerusalem, and it will fill the whole earth. This city is where Christ sets up his throne. However, Jerusalem is not in one geographic location; it's a spiritual city. The Scriptures were written to portray the glorified infinite church in a way that fits our finite understanding.

Jesus said, "On that day you will realize that I am in my Father, and you are in me, and I am in you" (John 14:20). We will be in a glorified form, for "just as we have borne the likeness of the earthly man, so shall we bear the likeness of the man from heaven" (1 Cor. 15:49). The millennial rule of Jesus and his saints will be a time of teaching. This will be a time of shepherding the flock. All we have to do is look at the first manifestation of Christ on earth as an example of what the future holds; Jesus desired to gather Israel under his wings. Christ came as a teacher and a healer. He was a helper to man, guiding his followers on the straight path to glory, pointing out the pitfalls in life for their own safety. That will be the course of our governance in the new age.

The battle that now rages between good and evil is within the hearts of men. At this present time, Jesus does not force mankind to worship him. In this coming kingdom of God, the disobedient[172] and the sinner will not be forced to worship Christ either. Complying with the laws of the kingdom will still be a matter of choice. However, with the devil out of the way, man will soon recognize that God's blessing and cursing will be swiftly administered. The sinner will be accursed whereas righteous men will find divine favor. Mankind will learn to taste what is sweet and to leave the bitter dregs alone. Many of the wicked will choose death[173] over living in an age where righteousness abounds. Spiritual thorns will replace the thorns now manifest in our natural realm for those who strive against the spirit of Christ.

There will be 1,000 years of peace on earth. Yet this peace will not last forever. The devil has one more season ahead in which to deceive man. In this paradise, the multitudes of men and women who have populated the earth will be lacking in one quality: spiritual fortitude! God will provide a temptation at the end of the Millennium to bring these fledglings into maturity. Without such a day of adversity and a trial of their faith, these millennial Christians would miss out on what the rest of mankind throughout the ages has experienced; without the trying of one's faith, there can be no great reward. Also, this time of deception will be necessary to weed out the ungodly.

This next passage demonstrates that much of mankind will not be content with God's administration in paradise. Many will choose to follow the devil in his final attempt to overthrow the Kingdom. "When the thousand years are over, Satan will be released from his prison and will go out to deceive the nations in the four corners of the earth—Gog and Magog—to gather them for battle. In number they are like the sand on the seashore. They marched across the breadth of the earth and surrounded the camp of God's people, the city he loves. But fire came down from heaven and devoured them. And the devil, who deceived them, was thrown into the lake of burning sulfur, where the beast and the false prophet had been thrown. They will be tormented day and night for ever and ever" (Rev. 20:7–10).

It's interesting to note that Satan will gather a large following to rebel against the governing body of Christ at the end of the millennium—especially considering that this forewarning from Revelation will be proclaimed throughout the earth. Yet, if biblical history teaches[174] us anything, it teaches us how blind the eyes are and how dull the hearing is of men and women who have forsaken the knowledge of God.

## Their Worm Will Not Die

> "From one New Moon to another and from one Sabbath to another, all mankind will come and bow down before me," says the LORD. "And they will go out and look upon the dead bodies of those who rebelled against me; their worm will not die, nor will their fire be quenched, and they will be loathsome to all mankind" (Isa. 66:22–24)

The Lord is speaking after the manner of men, for we will not have bodies of flesh in the new earth. Let's examine the phrase "Their worm shall not die." A literal worm eating a carcass would eventually run out of food and die. This is a figurative statement depicting the loathsome condition of the ungodly. A worm never dying is an illustration depicting time. In the book of Daniel, it reads, "Multitudes who sleep in the dust of the earth will awake: some to everlasting life, others to shame and everlasting contempt" (Dan. 12:2). The good news is that those who have found salvation will awake to everlasting life.

## The Great White Throne Judgment

The next event in the schedule is the Great White Throne Judgment. This day will be the sum culmination and recompense of man's deeds. This will be a day when God is vindicated. No one will be able to accuse God of any wrongdoing. For the Christian, this will be a day of reward. God has not espoused us to Himself just to turn around and parade our faults before the entire human race. Like dross that is burned away in the fire, our sins are gone. Only the gold[175] will shine through for the Christian.

The unbelieving will finally believe! On this day, many fearful individuals will have serious misgivings about attitudes they've held their entire life—attitudes that have kept their hearts from seeking God, decisions they have made that have put salvation aside so they endure'" (Isa. 66:22). God is assuring us that He will never destroy the new heavens and the new earth.

Our present earth is a representation of the future realm God has for us. We will feel more at home in the New Earth than we do right now. Look at the Garden of Eden as an example. Picture the loving relationship Adam had with Eve, eating fruit right from the tree, basking in the sun in a beautiful garden, gazing down at the lakes and fields from the holy mountain, sleeping outdoors under the majestic sky, and fellowshipping with God in the cool evening.

Every wonderful illustration depicting that natural paradise and the love that was shared between Adam and Eve is an illustration of the divine Paradise and love God will share with us. Yet all of those earthly experiences will pale in comparison to what joy we will find in the New Earth. We shall be delivered from the corruption of death; we shall be free from the bondage of sin.

## The Feast of Unleavened Bread

Many theologians believe the feast of Unleavened Bread represents Christ's body and how it did not rot in the grave,[178] because bread without yeast lasts much longer than leavened bread. This understanding of the feast may have an application with Christians at the end of time: "Their bodies will lie in the street of the great city, which is figuratively called Sodom and Egypt, where also their Lord was crucified. For three and a half days men from every people, tribe, language and nation will gaze on their bodies and refuse them burial. The inhabitants of the earth will gloat over them and will celebrate by sending each other gifts, because these two prophets had tormented those who live on the earth" (Rev. 11:8–10).

Is it possible that our bodies also will not rot in death before we are resurrected and ascend? "But after the three and a half days a breath of life from God entered them, and they stood on their feet, and terror struck those who saw them. Then they heard a loud voice from heaven saying to them, 'Come up here.' And they went up to heaven in a cloud, while their enemies looked on" (Rev. 11:11–12).

This feast also has an application in the Christian's life: after finding salvation in Jesus (Passover), we feed on his teachings (Unleavened Bread). This feast represents us partaking of Christ and purging yeast[179] (sin and false doctrine) from our hearts. It also corresponds with the exact day God brought Israel out of Egypt.[180] The Children of Israel were slaves in Egypt. Egypt is a type of the world. God through Moses delivered Israel from Pharaoh's hand and through a greater Moses—Jesus Christ—has delivered us from Satan's domination.

## The Feast of Firstfruits

The Feast of Firstfruits is an illustration of God's early harvest of souls (the first resurrection). During this ceremony, the first sheaf of the barley harvest is cut and presented to the Lord. This symbolizes Christ: He was the first[181] to be resurrected. "But Christ has indeed been raised from the dead, the firstfruits of those who have fallen asleep" (1 Cor. 15:20). It also depicts those in Christ (the church): "But each in his own turn: Christ, the firstfruits; then, when he comes, those who belong to him." (1 Cor. 15:23). During this feast, the first of the crop's fruit was waved before the Lord to be blessed by God, ensuring a full harvest.

## The Day of Pentecost

The Greek word for Pentecost means "fiftieth": it means that there are fifty days from the Feast of Firstfruits to the Feast of Pentecost. Held at the end of the wheat harvest, this one-day feast is also called the Feast of Weeks because seven weeks pass between the two feasts. The numerical symbolism—seven days times seven—is that of completion to the highest degree. As far as the Messiah is concerned, it was on this day that Jesus "received from the Father the promised Holy Spirit" (Acts 2:33). Jesus is now glorified: he has completed the design God had for him. On the Day of Pentecost, God's design for Israel was also completed as the New Testament church was born. No longer was the gospel only preached to the literal descendants of Jacob. The Apostles soon realized that God had now granted the "Gentiles repentance unto life."[182] Perhaps this is why in the original feast, Israel was commanded to bake two loaves of leavened bread. Could the two loaves represent the Jewish and non-Jewish nations coming together to form one assembly? This may also answer the question of why He had them bake leavened bread (bread with yeast), because leaven represents sin and false teaching, which has plagued the church from its beginning.

## The Holy Spirit Comes at Pentecost

The Scriptures disclose a principle for us to consider, as shown in the King James Bible: "The day of Pentecost was fully come" (Acts 2:1). The Greek word for "fully" in the text, *sumpleroo*, means to accomplish fully, or fill up. In the Emphasized Bible this verse reads: "And when the day of pentecost was filling up [the number of days]." That saying demonstrates that the years Israel spent mimicking the spiritual event God was illustrating through ritual were now over; the real substance of Pentecost had arrived. On that day, as recorded in Acts, the Holy Spirit descended. It was the beginning of a whole new era for mankind. Pentecost was the day Joel had recorded in Bible prophecy. It was on this day the Spirit of God was to be poured out upon all flesh. This gift of the Spirit empowers the Christian to be a strong witness for Christ, as recorded in God's Word. "But you will receive power when the Holy Spirit comes on you; and you will be my witnesses in Jerusalem, and in all Judea and Samaria, and to the ends of the earth" (Acts 1:8). The feast day from the Old Testament that we call Pentecost had to do with a move of God's Spirit in the New Covenant—in this instance, at the very beginning of the church's formation.

Pentecost will have another, more perfect fulfillment at the end of this age. A look into Joel's original prophecy from the book of Joel depicts this Pentecostal outpouring of God's Spirit transpiring around the time of the sixth seal in the book of Revelation. Prophecy has applications in the church age at the end of time that fit the scriptural context better than their earlier partial fulfillments. In fact, Joel's prophecy will have its final fulfillment in the coming kingdom of Jesus Christ on earth.

Let's look at small portion of this prophecy: "And afterward, I will pour out my Spirit on all people. Your sons and daughters will prophesy, your old men will dream dreams, your young men will see visions. Even on my servants, both men and women, I will pour out my Spirit in those days. I will show wonders in the heavens and on the earth, blood and fire and billows of smoke. The sun will be turned to darkness and the moon to blood before the coming of the great and dreadful day of the Lord'" (Joel 2:28–31). This brings us back to the mortgage scroll in the book of Revelation, because when Jesus opens the sixth seal on that scroll, the sun turns to darkness and the moon to blood.

> I watched as he opened the sixth seal. There was a great earthquake. The sun turned black like sackcloth made of goat hair, the whole moon turned blood red, and the stars in the sky fell to earth, as late figs drop from a fig tree when shaken by a strong wind. (Rev. 6:12–13)

## The End-Time Harvest Will Be with Torrential Showers

Still reading from Joel concerning the harvest:

> The open pastures are becoming green. The trees are bearing their fruit; the fig tree and the vine yield their riches. Be glad, O people of Zion, rejoice in the Lord your God, for he has given you the autumn rains in righteousness. He sends you abundant showers, both autumn and spring rains, as before. The threshing floors will be filled with grain; the vats will overflow with new wine and oil. (Joel 2:22–24)

In the last days, the church will receive both the autumn and spring rains[183] at the very beginning of the growing season. Rain is a symbol of God's Spirit: this can only mean that as God's spiritual harvest is in its beginning stages, there will be a substantial outpouring of God's Spirit to nourish the crop to maturity.

## The Feast of Tabernacles

The Feast of Tabernacles is made up of the Feast of Trumpets, the Day of Atonement, and the Feast of Booths.

There can be little doubt that the ceremonial Feast of Trumpets from the Old Testament is an illustration of warning, battle, and victory for the church at the end of time. As the trumpets in heaven begin to sound, the war in the spirit will escalate.

Ten days pass between the Feast of Trumpets and the Day of Atonement. Maybe this is why in Revelation it reads, "Do not be afraid of what you are about to suffer. I tell you, the devil will put some of you in prison to test you, and you will suffer persecution for ten days. Be faithful, even to the point of death, and I will give you the crown of life" (Rev. 2:10). The number ten is symbolic of a time of testing in Scripture, and the Jewish nation is aware of this. During this time between holy days, Jewish people reflect over their transgressions of the past year and are of a repentant spirit. Yet this literal number of ten days is only a shadow of the real model.

## Then Comes the Day of Atonement

The Day of Atonement was the most consequential day of Israel's entire year. On this day, reconciliation was made for the sins of the nation—sins that could separate Israel from divine favor. God would either accept the blood sacrifice from the hands of the high priest or reject the offerings. Israel was commanded to fast.

On the Day of Atonement, Israel's high priest walked into the Temple past the holy place, beyond a heavy curtain, and stepped into the Holy of Holies, sprinkling the blood of a calf upon the altar. The Holy of Holies is an inner room where God's Spirit was manifest; it was in this room and with this blood that the high priest made atonement for the sins of the people.

> Only the high priest entered the inner room, and that only once a year, and never without blood, which he offered for himself and for the sins the people had committed in ignorance. The Holy Spirit was showing by this that the way into the Most Holy Place had not yet been disclosed as long as the first tabernacle was still standing. (Heb. 9:7–9)

The way into the Most Holy Place came with much struggle, suffering, and blood. Through his sacrifice, Jesus opened the door[184] for us. Now we are able to follow in Christ's footsteps through the heavy curtain into the Holy of Holies. The Hebrew word for atonement, *athalyah*, means "to compress"—the idea is of many becoming one. We could look at the English word *at-one-ment* to understand the principle. The whole purpose for mankind is to come into the image of God—to become one with our Father and His Christ. In the past, what held us back was sin.[185] When the true Day of Atonement comes, we will be cleansed experientially. On that day, something wonderful will happen—we will step into the true Tabernacle.

The Feast of Tabernacles or Booths was an Old Covenant observance that lasted seven days. At the end of the summer, when all the fruit from the harvest of the land was brought into the barns, the Hebrew tribes of Israel would offer various sacrifices unto God from the harvest.

This feast started on the fifteenth of October and was a time of thanksgiving to celebrate and praise God for the abundance of the summer harvest. God also had the people gather tree boughs and erect booths to dwell in during this celebration. These booths represented the booths in which the Israelites dwelled while in the wilderness when God delivered them from Egypt. Surely the Old Testament booths constructed of palm boughs were used for protection from the blazing sun. This Old Covenant ritual depicting protection from harm's way is showing us another ordinance with a New Covenant design: the church will rejoice in God at the end of the spiritual harvest in the hot summer season that lies ahead.

Our joy will be made full as we take our place at the great marriage feast—the Feast of Tabernacles. The harvest of the wheat will be in the barns. At this time, we will be enclosed by divine sanctuary into the ark of safety. As the wrath of God rains down, we shall be eating and rejoicing on the heavenly shore. Even as the children of Israel headed from their booths to Canaan's land, we'll be preparing to inhabit the land of Canaan, spiritually speaking. The Year of Jubilee followed these feasts in Old Testament symbolism. This was a time when all the land that had been forfeited throughout the years was redeemed to the original owners. The Year of Jubilee represents the coming millennial kingdom, with the Redeemer Jesus Christ taking possession of earth's domain.

It's essential that we understand what our fate is. Our fate is to be protected from wrath. Our fate is to be sustained through supernatural means, like the children of Israel in the wilderness, then received up into glory to the marriage feast at the end of this age. Christians need not fear the role God has for them. The yoke Christ has us wear will never chaff. Understanding God's calling for us brings about a desire in our hearts to fulfill that calling. We need to seek God's will, focusing on the knowledge the Scriptures contain, and stand as God's anointed.

God has hidden his most precious pearls of wisdom in the dark illustrations of prophecy. He is calling us to come into that knowledge that we might be fruitful. As the harvest of the earth grows near, it is written, "The winter is past; the rains are over and gone. Flowers appear on the earth; the season of singing has come, the cooing of doves is heard in our land. The fig tree forms its early fruit; the blossoming vines spread their fragrance. Arise, come, my darling; my beautiful one, come with me." (Song of Sol. 2:11–13). These are the days when Jesus brings in the firstfruit from the land.

# Chapter 14

# LAMPSTANDS, OLIVE TREES, AND WITNESSES

The book of Daniel and the book of Revelation were written in symbolism so futuristic that previous generations have never fully understood them. Daniel parallels Revelation in many respects; its final chapters go into great detail concerning Antichrist. Daniel saw visions and was told to record them, much like John, who penned Revelation. And just like John, Daniel was unsure what his visions were about. Daniel said, "I heard, but I did not understand. So I asked, 'My lord, what will the outcome of all this be?' He replied, 'Go your way, Daniel, because the words are closed up and sealed until the time of the end'" (Dan. 12:8 9).

As we see the time of the end approaching, the symbolism in these books is becoming clear. The Spirit of God is teaching us: "He who has an ear, let him hear what the Spirit says to the churches" (Rev. 2:7). The Holy Spirit is calling us into a deeper knowledge of the prophetic word. However, there are those who are fighting this instruction by staunchly adhering to end-time doctrines established in the last century. Many Bible-professing Christians are sure there is no need to adjust their theology—but what if this is not the case? In this chapter I will present strong reasons to show that certain aspects of our popular, yet dated, eschatology need to be revised.

Now is the time to look into Revelation's hidden mystery and see it appear as clear as water: "But in the days when the seventh angel is about to sound his trumpet, the mystery of God will be accomplished" (Rev. 10:7). Please note, a mystery was mentioned.

This mystery has to do with what God promised his servants through the prophets—an early resurrection from among the dead and eternal life for the faithful. We see this same *mystery* mentioned in a well-known and accepted Rapture text: "Listen, I tell you a mystery: We will not all sleep, but we will all be changed—in a flash, in the twinkling of an eye, at the last trumpet. For the trumpet will sound, the dead will be raised imperishable, and we will be changed" (1 Cor. 15:51–52).

Understanding Revelation's mystery is simple. Just connect the two mysteries in our texts, then add the qualifying factor that puts it all together: "The seventh angel sounded his trumpet" (Rev. 11:15). Now let's go back a few verses and see what happened right before that seventh trumpet sounded. The very thing God promised his servants came to pass with the words "Come up here"; that's what a loud voice from heaven cried out as "they went up to heaven in a cloud" (Rev. 11:12). People have missed the significance of this passage for years because they have failed to understand who Revelation's two witnesses are.

## Two Witnesses—What They Are and What They Are Not

First of all we should consider that the word usage in Revelation is figurative, leaving open the possibility that Revelation's "two witnesses" might be symbolic of something other than two literal men or women. Revelation itself tells us who the two witnesses are, "These are the two olive trees and the two lampstands that stand before the Lord of the earth" (Rev. 11:4). Earlier in the same book, Jesus was seen standing in the middle of seven golden lampstands. Was Christ standing among seven men? Not according to Scripture, where it reads, "The seven lampstands are the seven churches" (Rev. 1:20).

Understanding that in Revelation 1 Jesus was seen standing among lampstands, which represent churches, in chapter 11 of the same book, it's only reasonable to surmise that lampstands would still represent churches. Of the seven churches Jesus addressed in Revelation's letters to the churches, the last two were the church of Philadelphia[186] and the church of Laodicea.[187] Christ praised the first church and gave a strong warning to the second. These assemblies existed at the time John was penning Revelation. Yet they are symbolic of the men, women, and children who will be alive at the end of this age.

## Olive Trees in the Book of Romans

The two witnesses of Revelation 11 are also called two olive trees. The Apostle Paul explained in a letter to the Romans that the descendants of Israel, which are likened to a natural olive tree in Scripture, have now had a wild olive shoot spliced in—which represents the Gentile or non-Jewish believers. Paul was no doubt addressing this subject because many of the faithful in Rome were of non-Jewish heritage. Paul wrote, "Some of the branches have been broken off, and you, though a wild olive shoot, have been grafted in among the others and now share in the nourishing sap from the olive root" (Rom. 11:17).

That tree represented the nation of Israel. In this dispensation, all nations have been grafted into the symbolic tree that God planted and Christ cultivated. Olive trees throughout Scripture represent God's people. Churches contain people from both the original lineage of Israel and also from less noble descendants.

Some ministers[188] and authors[189] teach that Moses and Elijah will be resurrected from their graves and that they are the two witnesses/prophets of Revelation. However, let's consider that millions of people still living at the end of time who answer the call of God to abstain from Antichrist's mark and become witnesses for Christ may fit Revelation's illustration of prophets/witnesses.

## A Witness for Christ

Speaking of the nation of Israel, God stated, "*You are my witnesses*" (Isa. 43:12). In the New Testament, Jesus said, "And you will be my witnesses in Jerusalem, and in all Judea and Samaria, and to the ends of the earth" (Acts 1:8). Understanding that Revelation's two witnesses may represent a worldwide assembly of men, women, and children of both Jewish and non-Jewish descent who profess Jesus to be the Christ is the key to unlocking Revelation's mystery—because it's the two witnesses/prophets who ascend up to heaven in a cloud, when the angel speaks the command, "Come up here." (Rev. 11:12)

Yet much of orthodox theology scoffs at the idea of the church still being on earth deep into the days of Revelation's prophecies! Probably the greatest reason people believe that the Rapture will occur long before the plagues of Revelation fall is due to a misunderstanding of Revelation's symbolic language. While studying end-time theology, I've noticed that many theologians have their entire eschatology thoroughly established through reading the words of Christ[190] and the apostles long before they research Revelation. To further complicate things, by the time they do peruse Revelation's pages, their doctrinal positions have gained enough weight to steamroll over Revelation's meaning. Any illustration that appears to run contradictory to their established eschatology is simply reinterpreted.

The problem with this approach to biblical study is that it's exactly opposite from where one should begin. People should start with Revelation because it's the framework upon which every piece of end-time prophecy hangs. When Revelation's structure is used as a pattern, prophetic Scripture comes into harmony.

## Trumpets Are Given

We see in Rev. 8:1–2, "When he opened the seventh seal, there was silence in heaven for about half an hour. And I saw the seven angels who stand before God, and to them were given seven trumpets." Let's consider these verses and this depiction of the angels receiving seven trumpets, paying attention to Revelation's time frame. Among the most popular theories of Revelation's time frame is that the tribulation lasts seven years, with the Rapture occurring at the same time, or shortly before Revelation's first seal is opened. Yet the trumpets aren't given to the angels until the seventh seal is opened, which for all practical purposes must be years later.

## The Last Trumpet

"For the Lord himself will come down from heaven, with a loud command, with the voice of the archangel and with the trumpet call of God, and the dead in Christ will rise first. After that, we who are still alive and are left will be caught up together with them in the clouds to meet the Lord in the air. And so we will be with the Lord forever" (1 Thess. 4:16–17). In this text, which is the hallmark of all Rapture texts, a trumpet call is mentioned. When we examine a well-trusted parallel account of the Rapture, we discover that the trumpet spoken of in our Thessalonians text is called the last trumpet. It is written: "We will not all sleep, but we will all be changed—in a flash, in the twinkling of an eye, at the last trumpet. For the trumpet will sound, the dead will be raised imperishable, and we will be changed" (1 Cor. 15:51–52).

There's no question that this last trumpet is connected to the Rapture of the church, consisting of both living and dead Christians, because this is spelled out. Yet Bible teachers over the years have rejected the idea that this last trumpet in 1 Corinthians and the last trumpet to sound in Revelation are the same trumpet.

Because the implications of a seventh-trumpet Rapture are staggering. If it were true, that would mean Christians would still be on earth deep into Revelation's plagues. This would also mean we would be living on earth during most of Antichrist's reign. Many books on end-time events teach that Antichrist will be revealed to Christians right before the Rapture. In other words, we will know who he is, but we will be caught up before he rules the world. All of those who are certain they will be snatched from this earth seven years before Armageddon may suffer great disappointment if they are not. Many could fall from the faith entirely, not being prepared to face persecution.

Surely God has a path for his elect to follow, but it's not always an easy one. Look at what Christ went through during the crucifixion, and the Scriptures affirm that Jesus is our example. When Jesus prayed, "May this cup be taken from me,"[191] our Father's will was for him to go through that suffering. Speaking of Jesus again, the Scriptures read, "He learned obedience from what he suffered."[192] Our Father's will is for us to learn obedience also: "Dear friends, do not be surprised at the painful trial you are suffering, as though something strange were happening to you. But rejoice that you participate in the sufferings of Christ."[193] We shouldn't rule out the possibility that Christians may suffer persecution under the coming Antichrist system, especially when there is strong Scriptural evidence indicating that Christians will still be on earth when Antichrist is ruling the world. Here are a few examples:

1. "And I saw the souls of those who had been beheaded because of their testimony for Jesus and because of the word of God. They had not worshiped the beast or his image and had not received his mark on their foreheads or their hands" (Rev. 20:4). This group of faithful believers had delivered a

testimony; this same word *testimony* is used to portray the actions of the two witnesses.
2. Now when they have finished their testimony, the beast that comes up from the Abyss will attack them, and overpower and kill them" (Rev. 11:7).
3. This word *testimony* is also used to describe the actions of Christians in Rev. 12:11, where it is written, "*They overcame him by the blood of the Lamb and by the word of their testimony; they did not love their lives so much as to shrink from death.*"

In any legal proceeding, the purpose of the witness is to deliver a testimony. This word *testimony* means "to witness in a legal sense." There's another general word for testimony the Apostle John could have used that was not a legal term. God inspired John to record the legal term because all of creation is in a legal battle over a mortgage scroll. Our witness is a binding legal testimony that will be reviewed before the great white throne judgment of the Most High.

Revelation's two witnesses die for the testimony they deliver, but not every Christian who faces the new world order under Antichrist dies. In Revelation the church is seen from different perspectives—two witnesses are only one facet of her character.

# Chapter 15

# THE WOMAN AND HER OFFSPRING

A great and wondrous sign appeared in heaven: a woman clothed with the sun, with the moon under her feet and a crown of twelve stars on her head. She was pregnant and cried out in pain as she was about to give birth. (Rev. 12:1–2)

## Scriptural Indications of the Woman's Symbolism

The Woman is clothed with the sun[194]—Jesus Christ.[195] The moon is under her feet—Old Testament law and ritual. She has on her head a crown of twelve stars—Christians are promised a crown.[196]

The number twelve is used in scripture to illustrate both[197] Israel[198] of old and the New Testament Church.[199]

Stars are symbolic of people[200] and angels.[201]

Apparently this is an illustration of the heavenly church because the woman is illustrated with heavenly symbols (verse 1). The word *heaven* is used twice in our text—once to describe where the woman is, and another time to describe where Satan is (verses

1 and 3). And Satan, who is standing in front of her, has yet to be hurled down to earth (verses 4 and 9).

*The Concise Matthew Henry Commentary* spells out a feasible explanation of this prophecy: "The church, under the emblem of a woman, the mother of believers, was seen by the apostle in vision, in heaven. She was clothed with the sun, justified, sanctified, and shining by union with Christ, the Sun of Righteousness. The moon was under her feet; she was superior to the reflected and feebler light of the revelation made by Moses. Having on her head a crown of twelve stars; the doctrine of the gospel, preached by the twelve apostles, is a crown of glory to all true believers. As in pain to bring forth a holy family."

## The First Shall Be Last

We can be fairly sure that not every believer will be a part of the symbolic child that is born from the woman/church in Revelation's prophecy, because the illustration itself demands that a smaller body is brought forth from the overall church. Jesus said, "But many who are first will be last, and many who are last will be first" (Matt. 19:30).

One might wonder: On what grounds would God place one man last and another man first? On this subject it's written: "Fire will test the quality of each man's work. If what he has built survives, he will receive his reward. If it is burned up, he will suffer loss; he himself will be saved" (1 Cor. 3:13–15). If everyone received the same reward in the next life[202] regardless of how they lived in this life, then nobody could be saved, yet suffer loss like this passage claims. Some who have done less in life will receive a lesser reward than those who have done more.

As we think about what kind of reward God's faithful will receive, let's consider that the treasures[203] Jesus admonished us to store up in heaven are not tangible things. We may find an answer to our question in the words of Jesus. He said, "Because you have been trustworthy in a very small matter, take charge of ten cities" (Luke 19:17). Within the church, there shall be a ruling class, as it is written:

1. "If we endure, we will also reign with him" (2 Tim. 2:12).
2. ". . . until the Ancient of Days came and pronounced judgment in favor of the saints of the Most High, and the time came when they possessed the kingdom" (Dan. 7:22).
3. "Then the sovereignty, power and greatness of the kingdoms under the whole heaven will be handed over to the saints, the people of the Most High" (Dan. 7:27).
4. "You have made them to be a kingdom and priests to serve our God, and they will reign on the earth" (Rev. 5:10).
5. "And I saw the souls of those who had been beheaded because of their testimony for Jesus and because of the word of God. They had not worshiped the beast or his image and had not received his mark on their foreheads or their hands. They came to life and reigned with Christ a thousand years. (The rest of the dead did not come to life until the thousand years were ended.) This is the first resurrection. Blessed and holy are those who have part in the first resurrection. The second death has no power over them, but they will be priests of God and of Christ and will reign with him for a thousand years" (Rev. 20:4–6).

The last two passages spoke of priests. Priests in the Old Testament were the ruling class of Israel, yet they made up a relatively small part of the kingdom. Because Revelation is made up entirely of Old Testament illustrations, we may surmise that this analogy is showing us that not all of God's covenant people will share in this priestly office. Speaking of this subject, it's written: "And they will bring all your brothers, from all the nations, to my holy mountain in Jerusalem . . . And I will select some of them also to be priests" (Isa. 66:20–21). The words "some of them" are in contrast to "all your brothers." Christians understood this biblical truth in Paul's day—back then some of them "were tortured and refused to be released, so that they might gain a better resurrection" (Heb. 11:35).

## Two Resurrections

The Bible speaks of "the first resurrection."[204] A thousand years later, it speaks of another resurrection in which "the sea gave up the dead that were in it, and death and Hades gave up the dead that were in them, and each person was judged according to what he had done" (Rev. 20:13). The passage goes on to read, "If anyone's name was not found written in the book of life, he was thrown into the lake of fire" (v. 15). The word usage in this passage gives a strong indication that there will also be people raised at this time who do have their names written in the Book of Life. Apparently, these people have found salvation, yet they will have missed out on an aspect of Christ's kingdom in which he and his faithful servants rule over the earth for a thousand years.

## Revelation 12 Continued

"The dragon stood in front of the woman who was about to give birth, so that he might devour her child the moment it was born. She gave birth to a son, a male child, who will rule all the nations with an iron scepter"(vv. 4–5a). Please notice the term "iron scepter" in our text. Let's look into a parallel verse that also contains the words "*iron scepter.*" Jesus promised overcoming Christians, "To him who overcomes and does my will to the end, I will give authority over the nations—'He will rule them with an iron scepter'" (Rev. 2:26–27). By putting these parallel texts together, we may surmise that the male child in Revelation 12 who "will rule all the nations with an iron scepter" is an illustration of overcoming Christians. Nevertheless, some authors and ministers claim this male child is Jesus Christ, because elsewhere in the Bible, it's written that he will rule the nations "with an iron scepter."[205] And Jesus shall rule the nations as the Bible claims—yet so will those who share in his kingdom.

## A Male Child

On this subject of Revelation's male child, *The New John Gill Exposition of the Entire Bible* reads, "Not Christ, literally and personally considered, or Christ in his human nature, as made of a woman, and born of a virgin, which was a fact that had been years ago; but Christ mystically, or Christ in his members, who are called by his name, because he is formed in them, and they are the seed of the woman, the church."[206]

Since the church is illustrated as a woman in some scriptures, why would her seed be portrayed as a male child? A good possible answer is that in Hebrew tradition, the first born male was the one who succeeded his father in position, and if his father was a king, he was made ruler over his kingdom.

What troubles some Bible teachers about deeming this male child in Revelation as anything other than Jesus Christ is that it makes so much sense to them that it is Christ. After all, Jesus was a child at one time, and he was born of a woman. Yet there are certain qualifying factors in our text that will not fit this view.

An angel told John that events he was about to record would take place[207] in the future. The year A.D. 96 is commonly accepted as the year in which the Apostle John received a vision and penned Revelation's pages. If what the angel said is true, the events in Chapter 12 should be fulfilled after the angel spoke to John, not before! Yet Jesus was born over ninety years before John's vision. And this is only one of the problems with maintaining that Christ is Revelation's male child.

If Jesus was the child in our text, then the woman must have either been Mary or Israel. In the *Commentary of Jamieson-Fausset-Brown*, it's written, "The woman cannot mean, literally, the virgin mother of Jesus, for she did not flee into the wilderness and stay there for 1260 days, while the dragon persecuted the remnant of her seed" (Rev. 12:13–17 KJV). I might add, neither did Israel.

Let's look further into the context of verse 5. "And her child was snatched up to God and to his throne" (Rev. 12:5b). Jesus was a fully grown man when he ascended up to heaven; he was not a child. Yet our passage reads, "Her child was snatched up." In the original Greek language that Revelation was penned in, the direction to the throne is not the focus. Instead of saying her child was "snatched up," another possible interpretation could read: her child "was seized toward the throne." The *Emphasized Bible* by Rotherham states it this way: "Her child was caught away unto God and unto his throne."

This seizing of a body of overcoming Christians to the throne of God could have something to do with a change in the heavenly order. As Satan is cast down, a loud voice from heaven exclaims, "Now have come the salvation and the power and the kingdom of our God, and the authority of his Christ. For the accuser of our brothers, who accuses them before our God day and night, has been hurled down" (Rev. 12:10). The term "now" is indicating a specific point in time. Let's look at another passage that has similar connotations: "Then I heard a voice from heaven say, 'Write: Blessed are the dead who die in the Lord from now on'" (Rev. 14:13). Evidently, the words "from now on" also point to this time when Christ and his church take authority in the heavens.

## Revelation 12 Continued: War in Heaven

> Michael and his angels fought against the dragon, and the dragon and his angels fought back. But he was not strong enough, and

they lost their place in heaven. The great dragon was hurled down—that ancient serpent called the devil, or Satan, who leads the whole world astray. He was hurled to the earth, and his angels with him. (Rev. 12:7–9)

Usually, wars are fought over authority and dominion. This is what this war in heaven is about. As Jesus continues to break open the wax seals on Revelation's mortgage scroll, a battle commences. The position of authority and dominion that Satan and his angels once held is transferred over to Christ and his church. Satan and his angels are driven out of heaven. As they find themselves banished to the earth, and realizing that they have little time left,[208] they strike back at the woman's offspring on earth. "Then the dragon was enraged at the woman and went off to make war against the rest of her offspring—those who obey God's commandments and hold to the testimony of Jesus" (Rev. 12:17).

## Mental Gymnastics

Now that we've considered a balanced view of Revelation's twelfth chapter, let's bring into light a position that doesn't fit Revelation's general tenor well. Since the truth can stand up to investigation, let's give this doctrine a fair hearing. There are authors and teachers who believe the catching away of a body of believers to God's throne in Revelation 12 is the bodily resurrection and Rapture of the church. In order to maintain this position, one must perform some difficult mental gymnastics, because it's impossible to harmonize this view with the scriptural doctrine of a last-trumpet Rapture.

Here's another problem: those who claim that Revelation's illustration of a male child being caught up to God's throne is the Rapture also claim that the rest of the woman's offspring were unworthy to be taken, either because they converted to Christianity after the Rapture or because they were only lukewarm in their commitment to Christ at the time of the Rapture. Yet neither of these explanations seems adequate, because the word usage in the text points to a strong dedication to Christ. The rest of her offspring are described as "those who obey God's commandments and hold to the testimony of Jesus."[209] One might wonder, is this the type of people that Jesus will leave behind?

Let's consider another possibility—maybe these Christians have simply not arrived because the Rapture hasn't happened yet. And maybe Revelation 12 is showing us a contrast between the living church and those who have died. Revelation's martyrs "were told to wait a little longer, until the number of their fellow servants and brothers who were to be killed as they had been was completed" (Rev. 6:11).

## Revelation 12 Continued

> The woman was given the two wings of a great eagle, so that she might fly to the place prepared for her in the desert, where she would be taken care of for a time, times and half a time, out of the serpent's reach. (Rev. 12:14)

In verse 6 it's recorded that the woman/church had "fled to" the desert. But then later on, after Satan has been banished from heaven to earth, it's written that the woman/church "might fly to" the desert (verse 14). The words "fled to" in this chapter may be speaking of people who have already passed on to the heavenly realm. The words "might fly to" could be speaking of Christians who are still alive and might die in the days to come.

## A Solitary Place

The word "desert" in this passage comes from the Greek eremos, meaning lonesome; it can be properly translated "desert," "desolate," "solitary," or "wilderness." Some authors and teachers believe this desert is speaking figuratively of the United States of America and that Christians from all over the world will come to the United States for safety in this time of trouble. Others claim Revelation's desert is a literal desert on earth located "in Petra"[210] and that Jewish[211] people who have found Christ will go there to hide from Antichrist's rage during the tribulation.

However, Revelation's twelfth chapter is highly symbolic—it speaks of a woman, which is an illustration of something other than a literal woman. The sun in that chapter does not represent our literal sun. The moon, stars, and serpent point to things other than a literal moon, stars, or serpent. So we wouldn't necessarily violate sound methods of Bible interpretation to look for a figurative meaning for the desert in the same chapter.

The desert the woman flees to is called "the place prepared for her by God." Another detail surrounding this desert is found in verse 14: "The woman was given the two wings of a great eagle, so that she might fly." This type of word usage suggests a spiritual/heavenly application—it also suggests spiritual ascension.

## Revelation 12 Continued

From his mouth the serpent spewed water like a river, to overtake the woman and sweep her away with the torrent. But the earth helped the woman by opening its mouth and swallowing the river that the dragon had spewed out of his mouth (vv. 15–16). Water[212] like a river is an illustration of spiritual force. Could the earth opening its mouth and swallowing the river be another way of saying that Satan's spiritual force cannot get to where the woman is? We know that Satan has already been banished to the earth by the time verse 14 is mentioned, so here's a possibility. The solitary place the church will be protected in may be an illustration of heaven, and the pathway to this solitary place for many people could be through death's door.

## Revelation's Martyrs Died for Their Testimony

Please notice that the word "testimony" is used in verses speaking of Revelation's martyrs; here are a few examples:

1. "When he opened the fifth seal, I saw under the altar the souls of those who had been slain because of the word of God and the testimony they had maintained" (Rev. 6:9).
2. "Now when they have finished their testimony, the beast that comes up from the Abyss will attack them, and overpower and kill them." (Rev. 11:7).
3. "They overcame him by the blood of the Lamb and by the word of their testimony; they did not love their lives so much as to shrink from death. Therefore rejoice, you heavens and you who dwell in them!" (Rev. 12:11–12).

This last verse gives a strong indication that these people have died because the word "death" is used in the text—not to mention the word usage "rejoice you heavens and you who dwell in them." Many people shall die in the three-and-a-half-year period that Antichrist reigns. And when they die, their spirits will ascend to heaven.

In any war there are casualties. Looking into the history of the early church will demonstrate that multitudes died for the word of their testimony. Many were fed to the lions. Many were burned at the stake. Those Christians did not die in vain; they took a stand in life that had eternal consequences. They held the word of God high as a standard to be abided by at any expense. So shall it be at the end of this age. Once more God's people shall face persecution and once more multitudes shall die for the Christian faith.

When the winds of adversity start to blow and the driving rain falls in the early summer, many among us will grow to spiritual maturity; then comes the harvest. As we see events from the Scriptures unfolding in front of our eyes, the reality of biblical prophecy and the desire to follow Christ will set in.

These prophecies about the church defeating Satan and gaining access to the throne of God transcend finite boundaries. What the church is seen doing physically in the heavenly realm—taking a position of authority on the throne—she is also sure to be doing spiritually right here on earth.

# 144,000 OF THE TRIBES OF ISRAEL

In this chapter we will be looking at Revelation's mysterious 144,000 company. God seals this assembly of 144,000 men, women, and children on earth before any of Revelation's trumpets sound so the plagues will not hurt them; then later this same group is observed standing with Jesus on the heavenly Mount Zion. They are seen in heaven before the bowls of God's wrath are poured out, yet they are also observed on earth during the fifth trumpet plague, so they fit into the same general time frame as the group of Christians who follow the seventh angel's command to "Come up here." Because this group is apparently taken up in the Rapture at the same time as the two witnesses/prophets, the 144,000 may simply be another illustration of the Christian church.

## The Most Common View

Most ministers and Bible instructors presently label this 144,000 company as literal descendants of national Israel. One reason they do this is because in the book of Revelation, they are clearly labeled "the children of Israel"; even the names of the tribes are mentioned! If that weren't enough, it's widely accepted that all of the Christians will have been taken from the face of the planet in the Rapture long before Revelation's trumpets sound. So the general thinking is that only Jewish descendants who accept Jesus as Savior—becoming Christians after the Rapture—would be left to make up the 144,000. It's supposed that these Jewish descendants, after witnessing the Rapture, will realize the gospel message was true and accept Christianity. However, there is strong evidence to demonstrate that both the number 144,000 and the classification "Israel" are figurative[213] of God's children, regardless of their ancestral lineage.

## What Does It Take to Be "of Israel" in This Dispensation?

We know from Scripture that God is no respecter of persons, but will allow all nationalities into heaven. Our Father determines how to deal with his children not by the color of our skin or because of who our great ancestors are, but by decisions we make in our hearts[214] and the faith we have in Christ. While it wouldn't necessarily violate the general tenor of Scripture for a specific ethnic group to be singled out in such a highly symbolic book as Revelation, it would certainly open the door to a few legitimate questions. In a thoughtful attempt to solve this mystery, we should at least consider the possibility that the 144,000 are a multinational group of men, women, and children who are illustrated in Revelation as "the tribes of Israel."

Let's examine the Scriptures and see what it takes to be labeled "Israel" in this dispensation:[215]

1. The gentile Christian nations were grafted into the tree of natural Israel in a symbolic sense, as observed in Romans 11. Might not this indicate that Christians are now considered "Israel" symbolically?

2. "A man is not a Jew if he is only one outwardly, nor is circumcision merely outward and physical. No, a man is a Jew if he is one inwardly" (Rom. 2:28–29). This Roman epistle was written to Christians of all nationalities, ethnic origins, and skin colors. From this scripture we may understand that in Christ, people become Jews "inwardly." Apparently in this dispensation, being "Jewish in a symbolic sense" is a condition of the heart!
3. "There is neither Jew nor Greek, slave nor free, male nor female, for you are all one in Christ Jesus" (Gal. 3:28). From this scripture we may understand that there is no longer such a thing as different ethnic groups "in Christ." We are now all one.
4. "If you belong to Christ, then you are Abraham's seed, and heirs according to the promise" (Gal. 3:29). Abraham is the father of Israel.
5. Speaking of Jesus, the Scriptures read, "For surely it is not angels he helps, but Abraham's descendants" (Heb. 2:16). If we were to theorize that this expression, "Abraham's descendants," should be taken literally and not figuratively,[216] we would end up with a teaching which maintains that Jesus helps only Israeli people.
6. [Abraham] "is the father of all who believe."[217]
7. "That through the gospel the Gentiles are heirs together with Israel, members together of one body, and sharers together in the promise in Christ Jesus."[218]
8. "Therefore, the promise comes by faith, so that it may be by grace and may be guaranteed to all Abraham's offspring—not only to those who are of the law but also to those who are of the faith of Abraham. He is the father of us all. [17] As it is written: 'I have made you a father of many nations'" (Rom. 4:16–17). "Many nations" speaks of different ancestral heritages.

9. "For in Christ Jesus neither circumcision nor uncircumcision has any value. The only thing that counts is faith" (Gal. 5:6). From this scripture it appears that keeping the Mosaic Law is not the basis of our acceptance into the new covenant;[219] faith is what really matters.
10. "Neither circumcision nor uncircumcision means anything; what counts is a new creation" (Gal. 6:16). In Scripture, "those of the circumcision group"[220] is a reference to the Hebrew people.[221] The words "new creation" speak of being born again; so in other words, Paul is claiming that being a Jew doesn't count unless you are born again.
11. "I know the slander of those who say they are Jews and are not, but are a synagogue of Satan" (Rev. 2:9). This verse demonstrates that ancestry alone is not what constitutes being a Jew, figuratively speaking, in the New Covenant. Seeing that this letter was written to an assembly with diverse ethnic backgrounds and given the figurative word usage in our text, it's very possible John was not speaking of the ethnic origins of the people in the first place, but rather their faith and walk in Christ.
12. "For they are not all Israel, which are of Israel" (Rom. 9:6). That verse in Romans just demonstrated that blood lineage from Jacob is not what constitutes being "of Israel" in this New Testament dispensation! So then having "citizenship in Israel"[222] must be a birthright accomplished through the new birth. Evidently, any natural descendant from any of the original tribes cannot possibly be "of Israel" without accepting Christ in this dispensation. And if he or she has accepted Christ, the Bible says it makes no difference what ethnic heritage he or she is from, or whether or not any are circumcised.[223]
13. Speaking of the Israeli people, Paul goes on to say, "Nor because they are his descendants are they all Abraham's

children. On the contrary, 'It is through Isaac that your offspring will be reckoned.' In other words, it is not the natural children who are God's children, but it is the children of the promise who are regarded as Abraham's offspring" (Rom. 9:7–9).

14. "For there is no difference between Jew and Gentile" (Rom. 10:12).

## Old Testament Illustrations

In Revelation the word "Lamb" is used twenty-seven times in reference to Jesus Christ: "Then I looked, and there before me was the Lamb, standing on Mount Zion, and with him 144,000 who had his name and his Father's name written on their foreheads . . . They follow the Lamb wherever he goes. They were purchased from among men and offered as firstfruits to God and the Lamb" (Rev. 14:1,4). When the *Lamb* and the 144,000 of the tribes of *Israel* are observed in the same verse, wouldn't this demonstrate that both the Lamb and Israel are Old Testament representations of a New Testament design? If teachers of Bible prophecy would be consistent in their theology and use this text as a model to build upon, they would understand that the Lamb Jesus Christ is illustrated in Revelation with Old Testament symbolism and so is the end-time church. Don't let the symbolism confuse you.

## The Firstfruit That Comes from the Harvest

Let's contemplate the meaning of this passage that is directly linked to the 144,000: "They follow the Lamb wherever he goes. They were purchased from among men and offered as firstfruits to God and the Lamb" (Rev. 14:4). A more accurate rendition of the word "firstfruits" is *firstfruit* in a singular sense. If we look at the meaning of the text, paying attention to the expression *firstfruit* without any preconceived theology, it would appear that these redeemed people are the "firstfruit to God and the Lamb."

This is a symbolic verse, so let's look into what the expression *firstfruit* signifies. It's symbolic of the first fruit that comes from the crop at the beginning of the harvest. The symbolism comes from the Old Testament feast of first fruits. This spring feast celebrated the harvest of the barley crop that had been planted during the winter, which came to maturity before the wheat and the corn. During this feast, the first sheaf of the harvest is cut and presented to God. This symbolism of the firstfruit implies that this company of 144,000 has been gleaned from God's harvest first, before the other crops come in. "For as in Adam all die, so in Christ all will be made alive. But each in his own turn: Christ, the firstfruits; then, when he comes, those who belong to him" (1 Cor. 15:22–23). According to this scripture, the firstfruits are the first group of people to be presented to God after Christ's resurrection. Apparently, this group of firstfruits includes every Christian caught up in the Rapture from among the living and the dead. However, the 144,000 as seen in Revelation's seventh chapter have never died, so let's consider that their numerology could be just one quality that the total assembly of saints ascending in the Rapture will have. The numeric symbolism of 144,000 may be pointing to something other than a literal number of people—it could be pointing to spiritual maturity and/or completeness.

Some thoughtful person might protest that the very number 144,000, if taken literally, is too small for the total number of Christians who will ascend in the Rapture.

## Should the Number 144,000 Be Taken Literally or Figuratively?

Revelation's seventh chapter depicts 144,000 living people from the twelve tribes of Israel being sealed while on earth to protect them from the coming judgments; then in chapter 14, the exact same number are seen in heaven shortly before the bowl plagues are poured out. If these Christians are part of the first resurrection and Rapture, why didn't this 144,000 company grow in number as the multitudes of saints who had died were raised, ascending with them during the Rapture? This adds weight to the concept that twelve times twelve may be an illustration of the perfection of the church.

## The 144,000 As Observed from Scripture

The 144,000 are observed in Rev. 7:3–8 and also 14:1–5. It is written, "Do not harm the land or the sea or the trees until we put a seal on the foreheads of the servants of our God. Then I heard the number of those who were sealed: 144,000 from all the tribes of Israel. From the tribe of Judah 12,000 were sealed, from the tribe of Reuben 12,000, from the tribe of Gad 12,000, from the tribe of Asher 12,000, from the tribe of Naphtali 12,000, from the tribe of Manasseh 12,000, from the tribe of Simeon 12,000, from the tribe of Levi 12,000, from the tribe of Issachar 12,000, from the tribe of Zebulun 12,000, from the tribe of Joseph 12,000, from the tribe of Benjamin 12,000" (Rev. 7:3–8).

## The Bride-City As Observed from Scripture

In Revelation 21, the bride-city is described. This bride-company of Christians consists of all those who will be caught up in the Rapture and will reign with Christ in his kingdom. She is also illustrated as "Jerusalem," meaning "the city of peace."

"'Come, I will show you the bride, the wife of the Lamb.' And he carried me away in the Spirit to a mountain great and high, and showed me the Holy City, Jerusalem, coming down out of heaven from God. It shone with the glory of God, and its brilliance was like that of a very precious jewel, like a jasper, clear as crystal. It had a great, high wall with twelve gates, and with twelve angels at the gates. On the gates were written the names of the twelve tribes of Israel. There were three gates on the east, three on the north, three on the south and three on the west. The wall of the city had twelve foundations, and on them were the names of the twelve apostles of the Lamb. The angel who talked with me had a measuring rod of gold to measure the city, its gates and its walls. The city was laid out like a square, as long as it was wide. He measured the city with the rod and found it to be 12,000 stadia in length, and as wide and high as it is long. He measured its wall and it was 144 cubits thick, by man's measurement, which the angel was using" (Rev. 21: 9–17). The numbers twelve, 12,000, and also 144, used to illustrate the 144,000, are also used to describe this city. Even the names of the twelve tribes of Israel appear on her gates.

Let us look at a few parallel scriptures concerning the 144,000 and the bride-city. Speaking of the 144,000 it's written, "Do not harm the land or the sea or the trees until we put a seal on the foreheads of the servants of our God" (Rev. 7:3). And now a verse depicting the bride-company of Christians: "They will see his face, and his name will be on their foreheads" (Rev. 22:4). Something was written in the foreheads of these assemblies in both illustrations. The second passage indicates that the Father's name is what is written in the foreheads of the bride-city. That brings us to a third text: "Then I looked, and there before me was the Lamb, standing on Mount Zion, and with him 144,000 who had his name and his Father's name written on their foreheads" (Rev. 14:1).

The scriptural indications that the bride-company of overcoming Christians is one and the same as the 144,000 are overwhelming. The 144,000 have the same name on their foreheads as the overcoming bride. The 144,000 are observed standing on the same mountain that is lowered down from heaven as the bride. The 144,000 have the same exact numerical symbolism as the bride-city. The 144,000 are labeled with the same tribal names as the bride-city. The 144,000 are caught up in the same Rapture as the Christian bride. The 144,000 rule with Christ during his kingdom, as does the bride.

## Mount Zion—The Church of the First Born

In the Old Testament, *Zion* was used to denote Jerusalem,[224] Israel,[225] or God's people in general.[226] In the New Testament, the terms *Mount Zion* and *the heavenly Jerusalem* are used to represent the glorified church, as it's written: "But you have come to Mount Zion, to the heavenly Jerusalem, the city of the living God. You have come to thousands upon thousands of angels in joyful assembly, to the church of the firstborn" (Heb. 12:22–23).

Many different symbols are used to represent the church in prophecy: a woman, a child, lampstands, prophets, witnesses, the new Jerusalem, and Mount Zion. "The Lord roars from Zion" (Amos 1:2). The Bible is crying out to these Christians. Like wisdom, as it gathers its chosen ones together, even so Zion, the city of the living God, yea, the heavenly Jerusalem, is beckoning forth a welcome.

Chapter 17

# THE GREAT DISAPPOINTMENT

In the nineteen-sixties, the hippie movement swept throughout America, waving the banner of free love, drugs, and rock and roll. Timothy Leary was high on LSD, preaching his psychedelic message, "Tune in, turn on, and drop out," to our youth. Evolution had replaced the need for a Creator in our classrooms; science was replacing the need for religion in our minds. A headline in *The New York Times* read, "God Is Dead."

As we entered the nineteen-seventies, many "baby-boomers" began looking for spiritual answers. The apocalyptic message in a book entitled *The Vision* by David Wilkerson was selling in record numbers. Wilkerson had a vision in 1973 and he was determined to tell the world about it. His book forecasted a time in which "nature will go wild" with "drastic weather changes and earthquakes" unleashing their fury upon earth. By 1978 the Jesus Movement was in full swing; many were sure the end was imminent. In a 1983 New Year's Eve TV special, the well-known evangelist Oral Roberts predicted the Rapture of the church before 1990. But 1990 came and went; God's people did not ascend. Now we have entered the next millennium, and for many, the return of Jesus Christ is overdue.

## Advent Theology

In this chapter we cover the recent history of two men whose predictions have had an impact upon millions. Because of their teaching, religious laypeople to this day are parroting falsehoods. Studying the theology these men propagated is essential. It will not only steer us away from their false teaching, but also steer us from the thinking that has allowed this type of delusion to become so widespread.

## William Miller (1782–1849), Founder of a Movement that Branched Into the Seventh Day Adventists

William Miller was the eldest of sixteen children. He was a sincere man; he was a dedicated seeker of light, holding the highest degree of Masonry given in the region of Massachusetts where he lived. He became a Baptist preacher. Miller made it into the history books by predicting the year when Christ would appear and the end of the world would come. This alleged appearing of Jesus Christ became known as "the Advent" or "the Second Advent."

## An Insubstantial Beginning

In the 1840s, the Millerite movement was mostly confined to the northeastern United States. It did make it to Europe and Great Britain; however, Miller's teachings didn't have much impact overseas, possibly because there was a lack of apparatus for spreading Miller's message back then. The first public telegram wasn't sent until 1844, and the telephone wasn't invented for another thirty years.

Miller made it clear that he did not acquire his knowledge of the year of Christ's return through divine revelation. He claimed he discovered the "time" through a study of Dan. 8:14 and certain verses in Revelation. After exhaustively researching the chronology in Daniel for seven years, Miller was convinced that the coming of Christ was likely to occur about the year 1843.[227]

Miller was deeply moved. He came to believe it was his obligation to "Go and tell the world of their danger."[228] That is exactly what Miller did. On the second Sunday of August 1831, he started his public speaking ministry. The crowd that heard him became ecstatic. A huge tent was made. Soon Miller and his associates were preaching hell-and-damnation sermons to large audiences. They used the fear of Christ's imminent return to stir people up to the point of conversion. During the twelve years that Miller proclaimed "the message of the hour," he stated that he personally had given over four thousand[229] lectures.

## A Small Slip-Up

Miller taught publicly that somewhere between March 21, 1843, and March 21, 1844, a great trumpet from heaven would sound, Jesus Christ would catch up the faithful, and the wicked would be immediately destroyed by fire. That year came and went without the anticipated results. On the morning after the last possible day for the Advent passed, Miller was in despair. Obviously, there had been a slip-up. The wicked made it though the "Time" without a hitch. The righteous followers still firmly on the ground were greatly disappointed.

One of Miller's associates, Samuel Snow, pored over the prophecy in Daniel once more, looking for an explanation as to why the Advent had not come to pass. Snow soon figured that Miller was off by one year in his calculations. He believed that from the beginning of the decree spoken of in Daniel to rebuild Jerusalem to 1843, only 2,299 years would have passed. Evidently Miller had made a miscalculation, and 1843 would end up being one year shy of the 2,300 years needed to allegedly fulfill Daniel's prophecy. Snow was now certain that Christ would return on October 22, 1844, at midnight. Miller eventually endorsed this new date.

## On the Road Again

> As this new light spread among the Adventist believers, it seemed there was an irresistible power attending its proclamation . . . It swept over the land with the velocity of a tornado and it reached hearts in different and distant places almost simultaneously, and in a manner which can be accounted for only on the supposition that God was in it.[230]

Miller and Snow claimed: "There is no possibility of a mistake in this time."[231] They warned the unbelieving, "Those who reject this light will be lost." To the uninitiated, the signs of Christ's coming were too plain to be doubted. Magazines were printed, heralding the coming of Christ. Newspaper reporters attended and covered Adventists' speaking engagements. Fifteen hundred Millerites traveled across the United States, going from town to town, proclaiming "the Advent near."

When October 22 came, the Millerites watched and prayed. With white ascension robes on, many stood upon rooftops, anticipating a heavenly ride. As the midnight hour approached, the faithful were at peace with God. They spent the last hours in quiet solitude. Softly praying. Waiting. Resting. Standing on the brink of eternity. The summer was over; the harvest was in the barns. It was time for the laborers to reap their rewards. Now was the time to flee from Egypt and enter Canaan's land. Now was the time.

Nothing happened on October 22. For the faithful, heavy depression set in. This day was perhaps the greatest disappointment to befall the church in the history of the New Dispensation. Fifty thousand of Miller's followers had found it impossible to stay in fellowship with their former congregations. They left those churches when their peers failed to accept William Miller's delusion. These fifty thousand now had to face the truth. They hadn't been taken into glory. The wicked still weren't destroyed by fire. One by one they retreated from their housetops and places of worship and went to bed.

Miller penned a letter for the faithful: "Brethren hold fast; let no man take your crown. I have fixed my mind on another time, and here I mean to stand until God gives me more light, and that is today, today, and today, until he comes."[232]

William Miller never accepted the new thoughts espoused by the Adventist leaders who took his failed prediction about the "Time" of Christ's return and tried to make sense out of it.

## Had There Been Another Slip-Up?

Could a movement that spanned twelve years and had over fifty thousand believers be wrong? The faithful had been living in a revival-like atmosphere for years. Many had quit their jobs and given all of their possessions to nonbelievers in the days before October 22 as a testimony to their faith. In the days following the Great Disappointment, the unwavering followers were convinced that this was merely the final test. Surely something significant happened on October 22, 1844?

## Does This Sound Logical?

Eventually the Adventist leaders taught that the computation of Miller's prophecy in Daniel was correct: they claimed that the 2,300-day period mentioned in Daniel did end in 1844, on October 22, at midnight, but they now believed Miller had made a few mistakes. The Adventists soon came to believe that Christ was not supposed to come to earth in October 1844 as first thought. They concluded that William Miller had made an error in the interpretation of Daniel's prophecy, not in the time,[233] but in the representation of the sanctuary, or temple, the prophecy depicted.

Let's look at that prophecy: "He said to me, 'It will take 2,300 evenings and mornings; then the sanctuary will be reconsecrated'" (Dan. 8:14). Miller had substituted the days in Daniel for years. Miller taught that Daniel's 2,300-year period started in 457 B.C., with the decree of Artaxerxes to rebuild Jerusalem; he simply added 2,300 years to 457 B.C. and arrived at A.D. 1844. He taught that the "sanctuary" in Daniel was the earth, but now the Adventists believed it was not. Miller had taught that when the sanctuary, or earth, was cleansed, Christ would return; now his associates believed he would not. The Adventists came to believe that when God gave Moses the pattern for the tabernacle in the Old Testament, it was the representation[234] of a heavenly temple, or sanctuary.

## New Light—A New Understanding of Daniel's Vision

It's recorded in the Old Testament that Israel's high priest entered the Holy of Holies in the temple once a year to make intercession for the sins of Israel. It's also written in the New Covenant that Jesus now holds the position of high priest. The Old Covenant design of the high priest making atonement for man's sins was fulfilled in Jesus Christ. Building upon this model, the Adventists began to teach that even as the earthly high priest entered an earthly temple on the Day of Atonement, on October 22, 1844, the heavenly High Priest—Jesus—stepped through the heavenly temple's[235] veil, moving from the holy place to the Holy of Holies. Having entered the most holy place in the heavenly temple, Christ had now, as of October 22, 1844, at midnight, allegedly cleansed the sanctuary in fulfillment of Daniel's prophecy. This is the position of the Seventh-Day Adventists today.[236]

## The Millerite Movement Splits into Factions

Others rejected this concept, believing that Jesus Christ had returned to earth on October 22, 1844, and that he is invisible. This division believed the world did come to an end; however, the end happened differently than they expected. There were many theories as to when Christ's kingdom would be ushered in. One maintained it would take an additional three and one-half years after Christ's invisible return before his kingdom would be thoroughly established, which led to setting another date in 1848.

## Adventism—Atmosphere of the Time

William Miller's ministry had produced fruit in such people as Brother George Storrs, Joshua V. Himes, Ellen G. White, and Nelson H. Barbour. These men and women kept the Advent faith alive. The Seventh-Day Adventist prophetess Ellen White said: "Some are looking too far off for the coming of the Lord. Time has continued a few years longer than expected; therefore they think it may continue a few years more, and in this way their minds are being led from present truth . . . In a view given June 27, 1850, my accompanying angel said, Time is almost finished, get ready, get ready, get ready."[237] Advent fever was not going away. Ellen and her husband fanned the fire for years. The number of Adventists were growing steadily at the time our next subject was coming of age.

## Charles Taze Russell (1852–1916), Founder of a Movement that Branched Into the Jehovah's Witnesses

In 1868 young Charles Russell accidentally stumbled into a dusty hall where Adventist preacher Jonas Wendell was holding a meeting. Wendell proclaimed that in 1873, six thousand years would have passed since the creation of Adam. In the autumn of 1873, the Advent would occur, and the world would be destroyed by fire.[238] Wendell used a different method than Miller to come up with this new chronology.

Russell's faith in God and belief in the Bible, which had lapsed in recent years, were restored during this meeting. Russell began to fellowship with Adventist preacher George Storrs.

Storrs, one of Wendell's associates, had played a major role in the Millerite movement. However, Storrs became disillusioned with Miller after the Great Disappointment of 1844. He believed that he had been mesmerized by Millerite emotionalism. George Storrs took the young Russell under his wing and had a great influence on him. It was Storrs who taught Russell many of the doctrines that are penned throughout *Watchtower* publications. Among these doctrines are the following:

1. An earthly second resurrection for all those who had died without the knowledge of Christ;
2. A restored Paradise on earth;
3. The taking of the sacraments only once a year.

Many of Russell's ideas concerning the return of Jesus Christ and the coming kingdom came from concepts that were popular in his time. The two-stage return of Christ doctrine is a good example. Dr. Joseph Seiss refined the doctrine, which had originated in 1828 and spread throughout Great Britain in the 1860s and 1870s.

## Russell's First Publication

In the 1870s Russell began composing his thoughts on paper. In 1877 he authored and printed 50,000 copies of a 64 page pamphlet entitled *The Object and Manner of Our Lord's Return*. Many of the concepts stated in the pamphlet appear to have come directly from Storrs and Seiss. Russell also borrowed directly from the commentaries of Sir Isaac Newton and Adam Clarke.

While Russell gave no date for the return of Christ in this pamphlet, he did spell out the manner in which Jesus Christ would return. Here is a small sample:

"Briefly stated, we believe the scriptures to teach, that, at His coming and for a time after He has come, He will remain invisible; afterward manifesting or showing Himself in judgments and various forms, so that "every eye shall see Him."

In a footnote on the same page Russell goes on to explain,

"This scripture (Revelation 1:7) does not necessarily teach that every eye will see Him at the *same moment*" (Object and Manner, p. 39).

In this pamphlet, Russell stated that Jesus would return to earth invisibly with only his elect knowing of his presence; during the time of Christ's presence, the Rapture would occur, and then the world would be immediately destroyed by fire.

## Nelson Barbour Prints Herald of the Morning

In the 1870s Dr. Nelson H. Barbour, an Adventist preacher who had been with Miller, was printing a struggling publication entitled *Herald of the Morning* out of Rochester, New York. Barbour was a friend and colleague of George Storrs and Jonas Wendell. According to Barbour's publication, Jesus had returned to earth invisibly in 1874, and the Rapture would occur in 1878.

One winter's day in January 1876, Charles Russell read a copy of *Herald of the Morning*. Can you imagine Russell's emotions as he contemplated that the invisible return of Christ had already commenced. Russell had read *Herald of the Morning* shortly before his own pamphlet was published. Some sources claim that Russell first learned of the idea of a "presence" of Christ only after reading Barbour's publication. One thing is clear; Nelson Barbour's teaching on the return of Christ had a major impact on Russell's faith.

## Russell Backs the Publication Herald of the Morning

Russell sent train fare to Barbour and asked him to come to Philadelphia and fully show the scriptural proof that Jesus was present. This is exactly what Nelson Barbour did. Russell was satisfied with the reasoning. He moved to New York, backed the publication financially, and went to work as Barbour's assistant in publishing *Herald of the Morning*.

## The Disappointment of 1878

Envision Russell's frustration as 1878 was coming to an end. He had fully expected to be taken to heaven. Again, Charles was looking for answers. Charles Russell and Nelson Barbour had a falling out when the Rapture did not occur in 1878, because Barbour set out to change the date. Russell maintained that 1878 was the right year, but his expectations as to what would occur must have been wrong. Perhaps the resurrection was invisible. Russell surmised that the faithful who died after the autumn of 1878 would be immediately resurrected and not sleep in death. Russell believed that the dead were resurrected in 1878 and that the living would be caught up in 1881. Because of this and other disputes, Barbour and Russell split. Charles was now free to publish his own concepts: he started printing a bi-monthly publication entitled *Zion's Watch Tower and Herald of Christ's Presence*.

Russell penned these words:

Looking back to 1871, we see that many of our company were what are known as Second Adventists, and the light they held, briefly stated, was that there would be a second advent of Jesus—that he would come to bless and immortalize the saints, to judge the world and to burn up the world and all the wicked. This, they claimed, would occur in 1873 because the 6,000 years from the creation of Adam were complete then.

Well, 1873 came, the end of 6,000 years, and yet no burning of the world; but prophecies were found which pointed positively

## The Great Disappointment

to 1874 as the time when Jesus was due to be present . . . The autumn of 1874 anxiously expected finally came, but the earth rolled on as ever; "all things continued as they were from the beginning of creation." All their hearts were sad; they said, surely we have been in error—but where? Surely it is clearly taught that Jesus will come again; perhaps our calculation of time is at fault. Carefully they examined the chronology but it seemed faultless and positively declared that the 6,000 years ended in 1873. Then the prophetic arguments were carefully re-examined: Was an error found? No, they stood the test of all investigation. ("Cast Not Away Therefore Your Confidence," Zion's Watchtower, Feb. 1881)

Russell was convinced that the period that he and his colleagues set for Christ's presence to begin on earth was correct. However, as the year 1881 was coming to an end, he found it necessary to make some changes in his timetable. Russell abandoned the earlier time frames of a three-and-a-half- or seven-year period after Christ's invisible return before the world would experience Armageddon and started teaching there would be a forty-year waiting period[239] instead.

In due time the Watchtower Society maintained that Armageddon would occur in the autumn of 1914. 1914 came and went. Russell then penned these words: "We consider it an established truth that the final end of the kingdoms of this world, and the full establishment of the kingdom of God, will be accomplished near the end of A.D. 1915."[240] Russell also taught that the burning of the world by fire at Armageddon was no longer expected to be "literal in nature but was really symbolic and signified a great time of trouble which would be the close of the Gospel age and dawn of the Millennial age in which all evil principles of governments and society would be manifested and destroyed."[241] When Charles Russell died in 1916, he was convinced that World War I[242] would soon culminate in Armageddon.

After Russell's death, the Watchtower organization, under Russell's successor, Judge Rutherford, announced, "The establishment of the Kingdom in Palestine will probably be in 1925, ten years later than we once calculated."[243] Nineteen twenty-five came and went. Armageddon didn't happen. God's kingdom was seemingly nowhere in sight. The wicked were still among us. There had been one slip-up after another in the organization's date-setting practices. Yet, concerning the 1925 date, Judge Rutherford had once promised the faithful, "There will be no slip-up!" (*Watchtower*, Oct. 15, 1917, p. 6157)

## Claims Made by the Watchtower

In the 1920s, The Watchtower Society penned the following statements: "The indisputable facts, therefore, show that the 'time of the end' began in 1799; that the Lord's second presence began in 1874."[244] "Surely there is not the slightest room for doubt in the mind of a truly consecrated child of God that the Lord Jesus is present and has been since 1874."[245] Look at the word usage in these passages: "indisputable facts," "not the slightest room for doubt." These strong statements allegedly nailed down the Watchtower's foundational teaching that in 1874, Christ's earthly presence began. Earlier—in Russell's day—the terms "unchallenged and incontrovertible"[246] were used to defend this teaching.

However, as year after year went by, failing to bring Armageddon, followers were beginning to lose faith in the Watchtower organization. The faithful were leaving by the droves. Something had to be done. In 1932 a group of men at the Watchtower headquarters in New York restructured their timetable. They abandoned the 1874 date for Christ's invisible return altogether. Once again the year 1914 was in vogue, not for Armageddon, as was previously taught—1914 became the new year for Christ's invisible return.[247] The story as told in the *Watch Tower* magazine was that "invisible angels channeled"[248] this information to those overseeing the Watchtower organization. A Watchtower book entitled, *God's Kingdom* (1973) claimed this change was made official in 1943. This change in the time of Christ's return pushed Armageddon off for one more generation.

## The Great Disappointment of 1975

The Jehovah's Witnesses expected that as God's Seventh Day commenced, the millennial kingdom would be established on earth. In 1966, the year 1975[249] was officially embraced as the last year marking the end of the six-thousand-year period since the creation of Adam, not 1872[250] or 1873[251] or 1972[252] as was once taught. Many Jehovah's Witnesses, upon hearing that 1975[253] was the end of the great six days of human existence, sold their houses, quit their jobs, and went into the ministry full time. Older Witnesses withdrew their pensions and followed suit. The church encouraged this behavior: "Yes, the end of this system is so very near! Is that not reason to increase our activity?... Reports are heard of brothers selling their homes and property and planning to finish out the rest of their days in this old system in the pioneer service. Certainly this is a fine way to spend the short time remaining before the wicked world's end."[254]

These dedicated Witnesses expected that in 1975 or shortly thereafter, Armageddon would destroy all of mankind except for Jehovah's Witnesses. Therefore, Jehovah's Witnesses, out of a genuine concern, warned the world of their danger. From 1968 to 1975, the Watchtower Society grew in numbers by over two and one-half million.

However, when October 1975 came and went, it brought great disappointment to many who had trusted in the Watchtower organization and had sacrificed everything in order to win souls. Jehovah's Witnesses repeated the Millerite movement of 1844 in 1975.

Can we learn from the history of Miller, Wendell, Barbour, Russell, and the Watchtower organization? All of the years[255] these people established for the Rapture of the church, the Battle of Armageddon, and the Second Coming of Jesus Christ were erroneous, even though they were presumed to be infallible. History is bound to repeat itself. Therefore, it's inevitable that as the days pass before the actual Second Advent, certain men and women will draw multitudes to themselves by crying out, "I know the Time."

*For a very straightforward and informative history of two fundamental Watchtower claims, and how these claims fall short of the Truth, please go to the author's website, Richkelsey.org and click on the link, Two Claims of Jehovah's Witnesses Examined.*

# Chapter 18

# THROUGH THE DOOR AND INTO HIS IMAGE

It's written, "God is love."[256] As Christians, we have the wonderful opportunity to enjoy an eternal companion who will never mistreat us. A bad word will never be spoken. God has our best interests in mind. The eternal paradise our Creator has in store for us is worth more than any suffering we may go through down here. To sense His character, all we need to do is look into our own hearts because we were created in His image. The way we lovingly treat a spouse is a model of the spiritual relationship we will one day share with God in paradise. With the devil out of the way and sin no longer hindering us and the curse we now suffer rescinded, we will experience the wonderful eternal life that God intended. For some of us, we need to do a little soul-searching and pray a simple prayer to ensure that we find this life.

In the Old Testament book of Isaiah the Father is pleading with us: "'Come now, let us reason together,' says the LORD. 'Though your sins are like scarlet, they shall be as white as snow; though they are red as crimson, they shall be like wool'" (Isa. 1:18). God understands that "all have sinned."[257] He wants us to understand our need for redemption. Look at the opening words to our text:

"Come now." What other option do we have? Our heavenly Father desires us to step into the legal position Christ's sacrifice has made possible. Jesus cried out, "I am the gate; whoever enters through me will be saved" (John 10:9). Jesus himself never sinned, yet he allowed himself to be tortured and killed as a blood-atonement for us. He willingly went through that suffering for our redemption.[258] However, if we choose not to come through the door of Christ into the saving grace of God, we will remain in sin in a legal sense, bearing the weight of our own transgressions on the day of judgment. Without Christ, "it is a dreadful thing to fall into the hands of the living God" (Heb. 10:31).

There is no work we can do to bring salvation to ourselves other than accept Jesus as Savior. He paid the price of our salvation when he was put to death on the cross. God may expect more from us after we have been weaned from the milk[259] of His Word, when we are ready for stronger meat. However, the seed[260] must first be conceived—we must be born again before we can grow.[261]

A simple prayer is all that is necessary for us to step from sure death into eternal life and have all of our sins washed away. With one prayer, we can have Christ's righteousness imputed to us. When we pray this salvation prayer, we step into the new covenant[262] in Christ's blood. That gives us certain promises. One of these promises is that our sins will be removed as far from us as the east is from the west,[263] never to be mentioned again!

Our transgressions (in a legal sense) were placed upon Jesus at the time of his death. "Blessed is the man whose sin the Lord will never count against him." (Rom. 4:8). Have faith in this promise. In the book of Revelation, Jesus said, "I stand at the door and knock. If anyone hears my voice and opens the door, I will come in and eat with him, and he with me" (Rev. 3:20).

If you aren't sure that you have salvation—kneel at the cross and repent from your sins. Pray this simple prayer: "Jesus, you gave your life to redeem me. My sins were laid upon you. You were crucified for my iniquity! I accept and receive your sacrifice. I claim salvation in the name of Jesus Christ." "Flesh gives birth to flesh, but the Spirit gives birth to spirit. You should not be surprised at my saying, 'You must be born again'"(John 3:6–7).

## The Beginning of Knowledge

Once we are redeemed through Christ's atonement, we are sanctified; that is, we are set apart as a clean vessel fit for use in God's house. As we seek the heart and mind of Christ, we become enlightened. We see the world in a new light. We have understanding that far surpasses the wicked—we possess true wisdom. The fear of the Lord is the beginning of knowledge. The fear of divine judgment[264] is the beginning of our journey. Then, as we progress in our relationship with Christ, the love of God moves our hearts. Perfect love drives out fear.[265]

If we fall into sin, we simply pray and ask God for grace. We pick ourselves up, turn ourselves around, and appropriate the grace (unmerited favor) we have found in Christ. The more trouble we have in our walk, the more grace God has to cover our transgressions. God knows that we are in a fallen state. God knows that our hearts are wicked. Nevertheless, He is asking us to mature spiritually and put away the deeds of the flesh.

Praying and confessing our shortcomings eases a troubled mind. It clears the path for an honest and open fellowship with Christ. A wise individual entering into a relationship with a spouse does not tear down their house with lack of trust and deceit; neither should the Christian with Jesus. Everything we need to walk righteously with God has been provided; if any man sins, we have a "mediator between God and men, the man Christ Jesus" (1 Tim. 2:5).

## Feasting On Christ

Jesus said:

I tell you the truth, unless you eat the flesh of the Son of Man and drink his blood, you have no life in you. Whoever eats my flesh and drinks my blood has eternal life, and I will raise him up at the last day. For my flesh is real food and my blood is real drink. Whoever eats my flesh and drinks my blood remains in me, and I in him. Just as the living Father sent me and I live because of the Father, so the one who feeds on me will live because of me. This is the bread that came down from heaven. Your forefathers ate manna and died, but he who feeds on this bread will live forever. (John 6:53–58)

Most Christians understand this verse to represent the new covenant[266] we have in Jesus Christ, with Christ's flesh and blood represented by bread and wine during communion. Christians partaking in this covenant are symbolically eating Christ's flesh and drinking his blood. While that understanding applies to this text, this passage also expresses a more profound illustration.

Jesus likened his person to the bread that came down from heaven. Israel ate bread from heaven in the wilderness for forty years. When the dew evaporated at the beginning of the day, a small frosting of manna was left. Israel gathered this bread from the ground. God was providing nourishment through supernatural means for His children. Christians are called to consume Christ spiritually in this New Covenant. We are to live by him. Jesus is the blueprint.

It's interesting that the manna/bread tasted like wafers made with honey. That's what the little scroll in the book of Revelation is similar to: "I took the little scroll from the angel's hand and ate it. It tasted as sweet as honey in my mouth, but when I had eaten it, my stomach turned sour" (Rev. 10:10). The volume of the book is written of Christ. Christians are called to feed on the Word; Christians are to feed on Jesus. We are called to partake of every aspect of Christ—his flesh, his blood, his suffering, and his death. The saying "you are what you eat" also applies in spiritual matters.

## The Passover Lamb Revisited

The Passover Lamb from the Old Testament is a symbol representing Jesus Christ. God spoke unto Moses and instituted the Passover feast. Every household of Israel dwelling in the land of Egypt was commanded to take a lamb and roast it with fire and season the lamb with bitter herbs. This lamb was to be consumed entirely by the people. What they could not eat that night was to be burned. The blood of this lamb was to be put upon the doorposts of every house.

At the midnight hour, the angel of the LORD would pass through Egypt, and those children who had been faithful to God's call would be saved from the plague that was to bring death in the land. The faithful children who had the lamb's blood upon their doorposts and had fed upon the lamb in its entirety were sanctified. These children were set apart from the disobedient ones. This is what God is calling us to do figuratively: we are to feed upon the Lamb of God so we might be set apart from the children of disobedience.

Please notice that this sacrificial lamb was to be prepared with bitter herbs. In like manner Jesus Christ was a "man of sorrows."[267] Jesus "learned obedience from what he suffered."[268] A servant is not greater than his master is—"Therefore, holy brothers, who share in the heavenly calling, fix your thoughts on Jesus, the apostle and high priest whom we confess. He was faithful to the one who appointed him, just as Moses was faithful in all God's house" (Heb. 3:1–2). Let us also be faithful in our calling. Jesus Christ "offered himself unblemished to God"[269] because Christ's life was a life devoted to holiness. That is what our Father desires from us: not an outward pretentious parade of holiness with ceremonial robes and images, but holiness that comes from the heart, manifested in our deeds.

## The Purpose for Humans

Envision our heavenly Father, sharing his glory with His angels, yet in His heart longing for beings He could experience a deeper relationship with. Because of His longing for communion with mature children, there came a day when He set forth to create humankind. It was out of love that God desired to make children who would love Him back sincerely. Our Father wanted His children to know with hands-on experience why they trust in Him. His desire was for sons and daughters who would love Him from the very depths of their hearts. That kind of understanding could come about only through learning.

God understood that to get genuine love back, He had to give His created children free will. He also knew that with this freedom of choice, some of the children—the disobedient ones—would not care for him. However, freedom is paramount in God's plan and the key to the success of the whole program. Our faith must be tested, decisions must be made, and what we do must have real consequences in order for us to develop the desired value. That value is to love God out of sincere hearts, knowing He has our best interests in mind and to never question that fact again as we grow in God throughout eternity.

Understanding that there are two roads one could travel, let's take the higher way. "Those who belong to Christ Jesus have crucified the sinful nature with its passions and desires. Since we live by the Spirit, let us keep in step with the Spirit" (Gal. 5:24–25). The Word of God is expressing that we are no longer to live[270] like we did before we accepted Jesus as our Savior. As a new creation in Christ through the new birth, our goal is eternal life.

# END NOTES

Chapter 1
The Mortgage of the Earth to Satan

[1] Job 38:7 NIV
[2] Gen. 1:2 NIV
[3] Gen. 2:5 NIV
[4] Gen. 1:28 NIV
[5] ". . . there is no favoritism with him" (Eph. 6:9 NIV).
[6] "God "will give to each person according to what he has done" (Rom. 2:6 NIV).
[7] "Are not all angels ministering spirits sent to serve those who will inherit salvation?" (Heb. 1:14 NIV)
[8] Rev. 12:3 NIV
[9] Gen. 1:28b NIV
[10] "Eve was deceived by the serpent's cunning" (2 Cor. 11:3 NIV).
[11] Gen. 2:16a NIV
[12] "(3) The eldest son succeeded to the official authority of the father" (*Smith's Bible Dictionary*).
[13] ". . . you listened to your wife and ate from the tree about which I commanded you, 'You must not eat of it . . .'" (Gen. 3:17 NIV).
[14] 2 Pet. 2:4 NIV
[15] Matt. 8:29 NIV
[16] Isa. 14:15 NIV
[17] Heb. 2:14c NIV
[18] "Ask of me, and I will make the nations your inheritance, the ends of the earth your possession" (Ps. 2:8 NIV).
[19] Jude 6 NIV
[20] "his life a guilt offering" (Isa. 53:10 NIV).

Chapter 2
My People, Enter Your Rooms

[21] This prison, spoken of in Isa. 14:15, is the "Abyss" of Rev. 20:3 NIV.
[22] Dan. 9:26 NIV
[23] 2 Tim. 2:10 NIV
[24] Rev. 21:8 NIV
[25] Rev. 6:10 NIV
[26] "Wake up, O sleeper, rise from the dead, and Christ will shine on you" (Eph. 5:14 NIV).
[27] "Others were tortured and refused to be released, so that they might gain a better resurrection" (Heb. 11:35 NIV).
[28] ". . . even in death the righteous have a refuge" (Prov. 14:32 NIV).

Chapter 3
The Invitation to the Great Banquet

[29] Rev. 3:20 NIV
[30] "Let us throw off everything that hinders and the sin that so easily entangles" (Heb. 12:1 NIV).
[31] Mal. 3:1 NIV
[32] Matt. 23:5 (a small scroll containing the law pressed against the forehead of the wearer with a headband).
[33] "In the same way, on the outside you appear to people as righteous but on the inside you are full of hypocrisy and wickedness" (Matt. 23:28 NIV).
[34] Matt. 23:23 NIV
[35] Mark 11:30–31 NIV
[36] "and be found in him, not having a righteousness of my own that comes from the law, but that which is through faith in Christ—the righteousness that comes from God and is by faith" (Phil. 3:9 NIV).
[37] "Israel, who pursued a law of righteousness, has not attained it. Why not? Because they pursued it not by faith but as if it were by works" (Rom. 9:31–32 NIV).
[38] "These people honor me with their lips, but their hearts are far from me. They worship me in vain; their teachings are but rules taught by men.' You have let go of the commands of God and are holding on to the traditions of men" (Mark 7:6–7 NIV).
[39] "My sheep listen to my voice; I know them, and they follow me" (John 10:27 NIV).
[40] Heb. 12:15 NIV

# End Notes

[41] Luke 14:15 NIV

[42] Luke 14:16 NIV

[43] (Luke 14:24, author's insert NIV).

[44] "the Spirit of him who raised Jesus from the dead is living in you" (Rom. 8:11 NIV).

[45] "I will live with them and walk among them, and I will be their God, and they will be my people" (2 Cor. 6:16 NIV).

[46] Rev. 19: 11 NIV

[47] Rev. 1:15 NIV

[48] Rev. 21:2 NIV

[49] Song of Sol. 6:8–9 NIV

[50] Rev. 20:5–6 NIV

[51] Song of Sol. 2:13c NIV

[52] "I turned around to see the voice that was speaking to me. And when I turned I saw seven golden lampstands, [13] and among the lampstands was someone like a son of man" (Rev. 1:12–13 NIV).

[53] "The seven lampstands are the seven churches" (Rev. 1:20 NIV).

Chapter 4
Seals and Horses

[54] "or my wrath will break out and burn like fire because of the evil you have done—burn with no one to quench it" (Jer. 4:4 NIV).

[55] "If anyone tries to harm them, fire comes from their mouths and devours their enemies" (Rev. 11:5 NIV).

[56] "After this I heard what sounded like the roar of a great multitude in heaven shouting: 'Hallelujah! Salvation and glory and power belong to our God'" (Rev. 19:1 NIV).

[57] Rev. 16:2–17 NIV

[58] "Then they gathered the kings together to the place that in Hebrew is called Armageddon" (Rev. 16:16 NIV).

[59] Matt. 4:8 NIV

[60] 1 John 4:3 NIV

[61] Zech. 6:8 NIV

[62] Matt. 3:10 NIV

[63] "But for you who revere my name, the sun of righteousness will rise with healing in its wings" (Mal. 4:1 NIV).

[64] "Arise, shine, for your light has come, and the glory of the LORD rises upon you. See, darkness covers the earth and thick darkness is over the peoples,

but the LORD rises upon you and his glory appears over you. Nations will come to your light" (Isa. 60:1–3 NIV).

[65] "This cup is the new covenant in my blood" (1 Cor. 11:25 NIV).

Chapter 5
The Midnight Hour

[66] "A stern-faced king, a master of intrigue, will arise. He will become very strong, but not by his own power. He will cause astounding devastation and will succeed in whatever he does. He will destroy the mighty men and the holy people. He will cause deceit to prosper" (Dan. 8:23–25 NIV).

[67] Rev. 20:1–2 NIV

[68] Rev. 13:4–14 NIV

[69] John 8:44 NIV

[70] 2 Tim. 4:3 NIV

[71] "This term, borrowed from the vocabulary of pagan religion at Rome . . . designated . . . members of the council of [pagan] priests forming the Pontifical College, which ranked as the highest priestly organization at Rome and, was presided over by the pontifex maximus" (*New Catholic Encyclopedia XI*).

[72] "As happened frequently in ancient times, a person who had achieved the heights which Augustus had was sooner or later furnished with a divine paternity. In his (Augustus') case it was said that a god in the guise of a serpent had visited his mother in the Temple of Apollo nine months before he was born." (*Roman Realities,* Wayne State University Press, Hooper, p. 341).

[73] "About A.D. 40, Caius Caligula issued a peremptory decree ordering the erection and worship of his statue in the Temple of God" ("The Abomination of Desolation," *On Line Catholic Encyclopedia*).

[74] "He was the first of the emperors to deify himself during his lifetime by assuming the title of 'Lord and God.'"

[75] 1 Cor. 8:6 NIV

[76] "The scope of the anti-Christian legislation of Decius was broader than that of his predecessors and much more far-reaching in its effects. The text of his edicts has not survived but their general tenor can be judged from the manner in which they were executed. The object of the emperor was not the extermination of the Christians, but the complete extinction of Christianity itself" ("Decius," *On Line Catholic Encyclopedia*).

[77] Eph. 2:8 NIV

[78] "Therefore no one will be declared righteous in his sight by observing the law; rather, through the law we become conscious of sin" (Rom. 3:20 NIV).

# End Notes

[79] The Edict of Milan (A.D. 313):

When I, Constantine Augustus, as well as I Licinius Augustus fortunately met near Mediolanurn (Milan), and were considering everything that pertained to the public welfare and security, we thought, among other things which we saw would be for the good of many, those regulations pertaining to the reverence of the Divinity ought certainly to be made first, so that we might grant to the Christians and others full authority to observe that religion which each preferred; whence any Divinity whatsoever in the seat of the heavens may be propitious and kindly disposed to us and all who are placed under our rule. And thus by this wholesome counsel and most upright provision we thought to arrange that no one whatsoever should be denied the opportunity to give his heart to the observance of the Christian religion, of that religion which he should think best for himself, so that the Supreme Deity to whose worship we freely yield our hearts may show in all things His usual favor and benevolence. Therefore, your Worship should know that it has pleased us to remove all conditions whatsoever, which were in the rescripts formerly given to you officially, concerning the Christians and now any one of these who wishes to observe Christian religion may do so freely and openly, without molestation. We thought it fit to commend these things most fully to your care that you may know that we have given to those Christians free and unrestricted opportunity of religious worship. When you see that this has been granted to them by us, your Worship will know that we have also conceded to other religions the right of open and free observance of their worship for the sake of the peace of our times, that each one may have the free opportunity to worship as he pleases; this regulation is made we that we may not seem to detract from any dignity or any religion.

Moreover, in the case of the Christians especially we esteemed it best to order that if it happens anyone heretofore has bought from our treasury from anyone whatsoever, those places where they were previously accustomed to assemble, concerning which a certain decree had been made and a letter sent to you officially, the same shall be restored to the Christians without payment or any claim of recompense and without any kind of fraud or deception, Those, moreover, who have obtained the same by gift, are likewise to return them at once to the Christians. Besides, both those who have purchased and those who have secured them by gift, are to appeal to the vicar if they seek any recompense from our bounty, that they may be cared for through our clemency. All this property ought to be delivered at once to the community of the Christians through your intercession, and without delay. And since these Christians are known to have possessed not only those places in which they were accustomed to assemble, but also other property, namely the churches, belonging to them as a corporation and not as individuals, all these things which we have included under the above law, you will order to be restored, without any hesitation or controversy at all, to these Christians, that is to say to the corporations and their conventicles: providing, of course, that the above arrangements be followed so that those who return the same without payment, as we have said, may hope for an indemnity from our bounty. In all these circumstances you ought to tender your most efficacious intervention to the community of the Christians, that our command may be carried into effect as quickly as possible, whereby, moreover, through our clemency, public order may be secured. Let this be done so that, as we have said above, Divine favor towards us, which, under the most important circumstances we have already experienced, may, for all time, preserve and prosper our successes together with the good of the state. Moreover, in order that the statement of this decree of our good will may come to the notice of all, this rescript, published by your decree, shall be announced everywhere and brought to the knowledge of all, so that the decree of this, our benevolence, cannot be concealed.

from Lactantius, *De Mort. Pers.*, ch. 48. opera, ed. O. F. Fritzsche, II, p. 288 sq. (Bibl Patr. Ecc. Lat. XI).

[80] "Although criticized by his enemies as a proponent of a crude and false religion" ("Constantine the Great," *Microsoft Encarta Deluxe Encyclopedia 99*).

[81] The Council was opened by Constantine with the greatest solemnity. The emperor waited until all the bishops had taken their seats before making his entry. He was clad in gold and covered with precious stones in the fashion of an Oriental sovereign. A chair of gold had been made ready for him, and when he had taken his place the bishops seated themselves. After he had been addressed in a hurried allocution, the emperor made an address in Latin, expressing his will that religious peace should be re-established" ("Nicea," *The New Catholic Encyclopedia*).

[82] "For a time it seemed as if merely tolerance and equality were to prevail. Constantine showed equal favour to both religions. As *pontifex maximus* he watched over the heathen worship and protected its rights" (*On Line*

# End Notes

*Catholic Encyclopedia).*

[83] "The substance of the bread and wine departs in order to make room for the Body and Blood of Christ. Lastly, we have the commune tertium in the unchanged appearances of bread and wine, under which appearances the pre-existent Christ assumes a new, sacramental mode of being, and without which His Body and Blood could not be partaken of by men. That the consequence of Transubstantiation, as a conversion of the total substance, is the transition of the entire substance of the bread and wine into the Body and Blood of Christ, is the express doctrine of the Church" (Council of Trent, Sess. XIII, can. ii).

[84] "There was scarcely a country in Europe over which Innocent III did not in some way or other assert the supremacy which he claimed for the papacy" ("Pope Innocent III," *On Line Catholic Encyclopedia*).

[85] Pope Innocent III, *On Line Catholic Encyclopedia*.

[86]

**Revelation 17:5:** "And on her forehead a name written—Whereas the saints have the name of God and the Lamb on their foreheads. Mystery—This very word was inscribed on the front of the Pope's mitre, till some of the Reformers took public notice of it. Babylon the great—Benedict XIII., in his proclamation of the jubilee, A.D. 1725, explains this sufficiently. His words are, 'To this holy city, famous for the memory of so many holy martyrs, run with religious alacrity. Hasten to the place which the Lord hath chose. Ascend to this new Jerusalem, whence the law of the Lord and the light of evangelical truth hath flowed forth into all nations, from the very first beginning of the church: the city most rightfully called "The Palace," placed for the pride of all ages, the city of the Lord, the Sion of the Holy One of Israel. This catholic and apostolical Roman church is the head of the world, the mother of all believers, the faithful interpreter of God and mistress of all churches.' But God somewhat varies the style. The mother of harlots—The parent, ringleader, patroness, and nourisher of many daughters, that losely copy after her. And abominations—Of every kind, spiritual and fleshly. Of the earth—In all lands. In this respect she is indeed catholic or universal" (*John Wesley's Explanatory Notes on the Whole Bible*).

[87] Pope Leo X: "The popes, like Jesus, are conceived by their mothers through the overshadowing of the Holy Ghost. All popes are a certain species of man-gods, for the purpose of being the better able to conduct the functions of mediator between God and man. All powers in Heaven as well as on earth, are given to them" (*The Complete Idiot's Guide to the Popes and the Papacy,*

Brandon Toropov, Alpha Publishing, 2002, p. 258).

[88] "(1) There is but one true Church, outside of which there is no salvation; but one body of Christ with one head and not two. (2) That head is Christ and His representative, the Roman pope" ("Unam Sanctam," *On Line Catholic Encyclopedia*).

[89] Rev. 13:13–14 NIV

[90] A Small Sample of the Word "All" in Scripture

"And afterward, I will pour out my Spirit on all people" (Joel 2:28). The Apostle Peter spoke of the fulfillment of this prophecy at Pentecost. Therefore let's look to our historical record and see how the word "all" in our text fits the actual event: Was God's Spirit poured out upon every living person who walked the face of the planet at the time Joel's prophecy was fulfilled? No! So evidently "all" meant all those who would partake of the event, and possibly all of who will receive of the Spirit throughout the ages. Yet in no way did this word "all" mean all in an unqualified sense!

"To you, O LORD, I call, for fire has devoured the open pastures and flames have burned up all the trees of the field" (Joel 1:19).

"Look at your troops—they are all women!" (Nahum 3:13).

". . . the whole world will be consumed, for he will make a sudden end of all who live in the earth" (Zeph. 1:18b). This prophecy is evidently speaking of the wrath of God upon the earth shortly before and during Armageddon. It also has an application at the end of the millennium. And, maybe this is the answer to our question? Because we know that all of the world will be destroyed by fire as God folds up this creation—however, in this dispensation the text demands that we use the word "all" in this verse in a qualified sense.

"In those days and at that time, when I restore the fortunes of Judah and Jerusalem, I will gather all nations and bring them down to the Valley of Jehoshaphat" (Joel 3:1–2). I understand "all" in this passage to mean all of the nations in the surrounding area—the eastern world. Could this simple formula be the answer to our puzzle?

When we run across word usage in Revelation in which "all" nations are illustrated, such as in this text: "And he was given authority over every tribe, people, language and nation" (Rev. 13:7), shouldn't we utilize the same principles in that text as we do in the Minor Prophets, and if not, why?

[91] Rev. 13:15 NIV
[92] John 16:2 NIV
[93] Rev. 7:17c NIV

# End Notes

[94] "I baptize you with water for repentance. But after me will come one who is more powerful than I, whose sandals I am not fit to carry" (Matt. 3:11 NIV).
[95] John 15:25 NIV
[96] Matt. 27:25 NIV
[97] Matt. 27:11 NIV
[98] John 5:43 NIV

Chapter 6
Trumpets—Sounding of Judgment
[99] Rev. 5:9 NIV
[100] "Death has been swallowed up in victory" (1 Cor. 15:51 NIV).
[101] "The beast was given a mouth to utter proud words and blasphemies and to exercise his authority for forty-two months" (Rev. 13:5 NIV).
[102] Matt. 24:36–45 NIV
[103] Acts 2:2 NIV
[104] Isa. 64:6 NIV author's paraphrase
[105] Rev. 17:15 NIV
[106] Heb. 2:10 NIV
[107] Rev. 9:11 NIV
[108] Ezek. 38:10–13 NIV
[109] Dan. 11:41–45 NIV

Chapter 7
An Invasion of Locusts
[110] Matt. 13:38 NIV
[111] Joel 2:25 NIV
[112] "Appoint a commander against her; send up horses like a swarm of locusts" (Jer. 51:27 NIV).
[113] Rev. 5:6 NIV
[114] Rev. 13:1 NIV
[115] Rev. 17:11 NIV
[116] Rev. 19:14 NIV
[117] Rev. 16:13–14 NIV
[118] Rev. 20:4 NIV

Chapter 8
The Final Woe

[119] Rev. 3:10 NIV

[120] "Adam, who was a pattern of the one to come" (Rom. 5:14 NIV).

[121] "Let him who does wrong continue to do wrong; let him who is vile continue to be vile; let him who does right continue to do right; and let him who is holy continue to be holy" (Rev. 22:10 NIV).

[122] "'Let there be an expanse between the waters to separate water from water.' So God made the expanse and separated the water under the expanse from the water above it. And it was so. God called the expanse 'sky'" (Gen. 1:6–7). Here we see water under the sky and water above the sky. Then God separates the water under the sky and dry land appears. The theory is that the water above the sky, in a form of a vapor canopy, would have never fallen to earth until widespread volcanoes drove enough ash particles up to the vapor canopy during the Great Flood.

[123] Exod. 10:23 NIV

[124] "Even to this day when Moses is read, a veil covers their hearts" (2 Cor. 3:15 NIV).

[125] Zech. 14:5 NIV

[126] Rev. 1:7 NIV

[127] "The deliverer will come from Zion; he will turn godlessness away from Jacob. [27] And this is my covenant with them when I take away their sins" (Rom. 11:26–27 NIV).

Chapter 9

Deception Is on the Horizon

[128] "You are a chosen people, a royal priesthood, a holy nation" (1 Peter 2:9 NIV).

[129] "Among them are Hymenaeus and Philetus, [18] who have wandered away from the truth. They say that the resurrection has already taken place, and they destroy the faith of some" (2 Tim. 2:17–18 NIV).

[130] Dan. 9:27 NIV

Chapter 10

The Overcoming Church in Prophecy

[131] Rev. 5:8

[132] Rev. 7:9

# End Notes

[133] "When he opened the fifth seal, I saw under the altar the souls of those who had been slain because of the word of God and the testimony they had maintained. (Rev. 6:9)

[134] "Then I saw a Lamb, looking as if it had been slain, standing in the center of the throne, encircled by the four living creatures and the elders. He had seven horns and seven eyes, which are the seven spirits of God sent out into all the earth." (Rev. 5:6)

[135] "The smoke of the incense, together with the prayers of the saints, went up before God from the angel's hand. 5 Then the angel took the censer, filled it with fire from the altar, and hurled it on the earth; and there came peals of thunder, rumblings, flashes of lightning and an earthquake." (Rev. 8:4-5)

[136] "Since the children have flesh and blood, he too shared in their humanity so that by his death he might destroy him who holds the power of death—that is, the devil" (Heb. 2:14).

[137] "He exercised all the authority of the first beast on his behalf, and made the earth and its inhabitants worship the first beast, whose fatal wound had been healed. 13 And he performed great and miraculous signs, even causing fire to come down from heaven to earth in full view of men. 14 Because of the signs he was given power to do on behalf of the first beast, he deceived the inhabitants of the earth. He ordered them to set up an image in honor of the beast who was wounded by the sword and yet lived. 15 He was given power to give breath to the image of the first beast, so that it could speak and cause all who refused to worship the image to be killed. (Rev. 13:12-15)

Chapter 11
Choose Your Battles Carefully

[138] "He who overcomes will inherit all this, and I will be his God and he will be my son. But the cowardly, the unbelieving, the vile, the murderers, the sexually immoral, those who practice magic arts, the idolaters and all liars—their place will be in the fiery lake of burning sulfur. This is the second death." (Rev. 21:7-8)

[139] "You said in your heart, 'I will ascend to heaven; I will raise my throne above the stars of God; I will sit enthroned on the mount of assembly, on the utmost heights of the sacred mountain. 14 I will ascend above the tops of the clouds; I will make myself like the Most High.'" (Isa. 14:13-14).

[140] "But woe to the earth and the sea, because the devil has gone down to you! He is filled with fury, because he knows that his time is short" (Rev. 12:12b).

[141] "And the beast was taken, and with him the false prophet that wrought miracles before him, with which he deceived them that had received the mark of the beast, and them that worshipped his image" (Rev 19:20, KJV).

[142] (Rev. 12:3).

[143] "'The waters you saw, where the prostitute sits, are peoples, multitudes, nations and languages'" (Rev. 17:15).

[144] "'The four great beasts are four kingdoms that will rise from the earth'" (Dan. 7:17).

[145] Daniel 7:4

[146] Daniel 7:5

[147] Daniel 7:6

[148] "And the devil, who deceived them, was thrown into the lake of burning sulfur, where the beast and the false prophet had been thrown. They will be tormented day and night for ever and ever" (Rev. 20:10).

[149] Rev. 13:13

[150] "Because of the signs he was given power to do on behalf of the first beast, he deceived the inhabitants of the earth" (Rev. 13:14).

[151] Rev. 17:1

[152] Rev. 17:2

[153] "For your Maker is your husband— the LORD Almighty is his name— the Holy One of Israel is your Redeemer; he is called the God of all the earth." (Isa. 54:5)

[154] "And I saw what looked like a sea of glass mixed with fire and, standing beside the sea, those who had been victorious over the beast and his image and over the number of his name" (Rev. 15:2).

[155] "'to open their eyes and turn them from darkness to light, and from the power of Satan to God, so that they may receive forgiveness of sins and a place among those who are sanctified by faith in me.'"(Acts 26:18).

[156] "For our struggle is not against flesh and blood, but against the rulers, against the authorities, against the powers of this dark world and against the spiritual forces of evil in the heavenly realms" (Eph. 6:12).

[157] "'Now get up and stand on your feet. I have appeared to you to appoint you as a servant and as a witness of what you have seen of me and what I will show you" (Acts 26:16).

[158] "He will cause deceit to prosper, and he will consider himself superior" (Daniel 8:25).

[159] Dan. 11:37 Author paraphrase

[160] Isa. 14:12 KJV

# End Notes

[161] Dan. 7:8 Author paraphrase

[162] "the devil, who has taken them captive to do his will" (2 Tim. 2:26).

[163] "The inhabitants of the earth will gloat over them and will celebrate by sending each other gifts, because these two prophets had tormented those who live on the earth" (Rev. 11:10).

[164] "'What do you want with us, Son of God?' they shouted. 'Have you come here to torture us before the appointed time?'" (Matt. 8:29)

[165] Isa. 14:16-17 Author paraphrase

Chapter 12
Paradise Restored

[166] Mark 1:15 NIV

[167] Isa. 35:1 NIV

[168] Rev. 22:3 NIV

[169] Gen. 5:5–14 NIV

[170] "But when this priest had offered for all time one sacrifice for sins, he sat down at the right hand of God. Since that time he waits for his enemies to be made his footstool" (Heb. 10:12–13 NIV).

[171] Luke 19:17 NIV

[172] "The spirit who is now at work in those who are disobedient" (Eph. 2:2 NIV).

[173] Jer. 8:3 NIV

[174] "For everything that was written in the past was written to teach us" (Rom. 15:4 NIV).

[175] "If any man builds on this foundation using gold, silver, costly stones, wood, hay or straw, his work will be shown for what it is, because the Day will bring it to light. It will be revealed with fire, and the fire will test the quality of each man's work" (1 Cor. 3:12–13 NIV).

Chapter 13
The Feast Days—Now and Then

[176] "Therefore, brothers, since we have confidence to enter the Most Holy Place by the blood of Jesus, by a new and living way opened for us through the curtain, that is, his body" (Heb. 10:19 NIV).

[177] "By faith he kept the Passover and the sprinkling of blood, so that the destroyer of the firstborn would not touch the firstborn of Israel" (Heb. 11:28 NIV).

[178] Acts 2:31 NIV

[179] "Therefore let us keep the Festival, not with the old yeast, the yeast of malice and wickedness, but with bread without yeast, the bread of sincerity and truth" (1 Cor. 5:8).

[180] Exod. 12:17 NIV

[181] "For those God foreknew he also predestined to be conformed to the likeness of his son, that he might be the firstborn among many brothers" (Rom. 8:29 NIV).

[182] Acts 11:18 NIV

[183] "See how the farmer waits for the land to yield its valuable crop and how patient he is for the autumn and spring rains" (Jas. 5:7 NIV).

[184] "Because a great door for effective work has opened to me" (1 Cor. 16:9 NIV).

[185] Lev. 16:30 NIV

Chapter 14
Lampstands, Olive Trees, and Witnesses

[186] Rev. 3:7 NIV

[187] Rev. 3:14 NIV

[188] "God hid Moses' body (on Mount Nebo) so that he could use him again for His purpose at the end of the world. Therefore the two olive trees and two candlesticks are unmistakably Moses and Elijah. God sends them again in the flesh to this world to witness of Jesus Christ" (*The Apocalyptic Prophecy*, David Yonggi Cho, Creation House, 1998, p. 177).

[189] "In determining who the two witnesses mentioned in Rev. 11:3 are, most biblical scholars have narrowed the choice down to either Elijah, Moses, or Enoch" (Jack Van Impe's *Dictionary of Prophecy Terms*).

[190] Jesus said, "There will be signs in the sun, moon and stars. On the earth, nations will be in anguish and perplexity at the roaring and tossing of the sea. Men will faint from terror, apprehensive of what is coming on the world, for the heavenly bodies will be shaken. At that time they will see the Son of Man coming in a cloud with power and great glory. When these things begin to take place, stand up and lift up your heads, because your redemption is drawing near" (Luke 21:25–28 NIV).

[191] Matt. 26:39 NIV

[192] Heb. 5:8 NIV

[193] 1 Peter 4:12–13 NIV

# End Notes

Chapter 15
The Woman and Her Offspring

[194] "In the metaphorical language of Scripture the sun is emblematic of the law of God, Ps. 19:7, of the cheering presence of God, Ps. 84:11, of the person of the Saviour, John 1:9; Mal. 4:2, and of the glory and purity of heavenly beings. Rev. 1:16; 10:1; 12:1" (*Smith's Bible Dictionary*).

[195] "His [Christ's] face was like the sun shining in all its brilliance" (Rev. 1:16 NIV).

[196] "I have fought the good fight, I have finished the race, I have kept the faith. Now there is in store for me the crown of righteousness, which the Lord, the righteous Judge, will award to me on that day—and not only to me, but also to all who have longed for his appearing" (2 Tim. 4:7–8 NIV).

[197] "I tell you the truth, at the renewal of all things, when the Son of Man sits on his glorious throne, you who have followed me will also sit on twelve thrones, judging the twelve tribes of Israel" (Matt. 19:28 NIV).

[198] "He got up early the next morning and built an altar at the foot of the mountain and set up twelve stone pillars representing the twelve tribes of Israel" (Exod. 24:12 NIV).

[199] Rev. 22:2 NIV

[200] "Those who are wise will shine like the brightness of the heavens, and those who lead many to righteousness, like the stars for ever and ever" (Dan. 12:3 NIV).

[201] "O morning star, son of the dawn! You have been cast down to the earth, you who once laid low the nations! You said in your heart, 'I will ascend to heaven; I will raise my throne above the stars of God'" (Isa. 14:12–13 NIV).

[202] ". . . those who have done good will rise to live, and those who have done evil will rise to be condemned" (John 5:29 NIV).

[203] "But store up for yourselves treasures in heaven" (Matt. 6:20 NIV).

[204] Rev. 20:5

[205] "He will rule them with an iron scepter" (Rev. 19:15, Ps. 2:9 NIV).

[206] Copyright statement: *The New John Gill's Exposition of the Entire Bible* modernized and adapted for the computer by Larry Pierce of *Online Bible*. All rights reserved, Larry Pierce, Winterbourne, Ontario. A printed copy of this work can be ordered from The Baptist Standard Bearer, 1 Iron Oaks Drive, Paris, AR 72855

[207] "Come up here, and I will show you what must take place after this" (Rev. 4:1 NIV).
[208] "He is filled with fury, because he knows that his time is short" (Rev. 12:12b NIV).
[209] Rev. 12:17 NIV
[210] (*The Apocalyptic Prophecy*, David Yonggi Cho, Creation House, 1998, p. 184).
[211] "The Jews who believed in Jesus will be transported by God to Petra" (*The Apocalyptic Prophecy*, David Yonggi Cho, Creation House, 1998, p. 186).
[212] John 7:38–39 NIV

Chapter 16
144,000 of the Tribes of Israel
[213] "But you are a chosen people, a royal priesthood, a holy nation" (1 Peter 2:9 NIV).
[214] "For all these nations are really uncircumcised, and even the whole house of Israel is uncircumcised in heart" (Jer. 9:24 NIV).
[215] Here is a list of eighteen titles used in the Old Testament about Israel which are used in the New Testament to describe the church. They are
   1) the Beloved of God
   2) the children of God
   3) the field of God
   4) the flock of God and of the Messiah
   5) the house of God
   6) the kingdom of God
   7) the people of God
   8) the priests of God
   9) the vineyard of God
   10) the wife or bride of God
   11) the children of Abraham
   12) the chosen people
   13) the circumcised
   14) Israel
   15) Jerusalem
   16) the Jews
   17) the recipients of the new covenant
   18) those on whom the Spirit is poured out.

# End Notes

Here is a list of fifteen Old Testament passages speaking of the children of Israel, which in the New Testament refers to the church. They are
1) Lev. 26:11,12
2) Deut. 30:12–14
3) Deut. 31:6
4) Deut. 32:36
5) Ps. 22:22
6) Ps. 44:22
7) Ps. 95:7–11
8) Ps. 130:8
9) Isa. 28:16
10) Isa. 49:8
11) Isa. 52:7
12) Isa. 54:1
13) Jer. 31:31–34
14) Hos. 1:10, 2:23
15) Hos. 13:14

[216] "These things may be taken figuratively" (Gal. 4:22 NIV).

[217] (Rom. 4:10 NIV).

[218] (Eph. 3:6 NIV).

[219] "The time is coming, declares the Lord, when I will make a new covenant with the house of Israel and with the house of Judah. It will not be like the covenant I made with their forefathers" (Heb. 8:8–9 NIV).

[220] Tit. 1:10 NIV

[221] "Circumcised on the eighth day, of the people of Israel, of the tribe of Benjamin, a Hebrew of Hebrews" (Phil. 3:5 NIV).

[222] "Remember that at that time you were separate from Christ, excluded from citizenship in Israel and foreigners to the covenants of the promise" (Eph. 2:12 NIV).

[223] "If those who are not circumcised keep the law's requirements, will they not be regarded as though they were circumcised?" (Rom. 2:26 NIV)

[224] (Ps. 87:2; 149:2; Isa. 33:14; Joel 2:1)

[225] (Ps. 51:18; 87:5)

[226] "I . . . who laid the foundations of the earth, and who say to Zion, 'You are my people'" (Isa. 51:16 NIV).

Chapter 17
The Great Disappointment

[227] "With intense interest [William Miller] studied the books of Daniel and the Revelation, employing the same principles of interpretation as in the other scriptures, and found, to his great joy, that the prophetic symbols could be understood. Angels of Heaven were guiding his mind, and opening to his understanding prophecies which had ever been dark to God's people. Link after link of the chain of truth rewarded his efforts; step by step he traced down the great lines of prophecy, until he reached the solemn conclusion that in a few years the Son of God would come the second time, in power and glory, and that the events connected with that coming and the close of human probation would take place about the year 1843" (*Cosmic Conflict*, Ellen White, ch. 13).

[228] (*William Miller and the Advent Crisis*, pp. 8–9)

[229] (Jane Marsh Parker, "A Wonder Book of my Children," *Outlook*, May 1908, p. 117).

[230] (*Advent Herald in Portsmouth Journal*, November 9, 1844)

[231] (*History of Advent Message*, p. 596)

[232] (Bliss, *Memoirs*, p. 278)

[233] "The scripture which above all others had been both the foundation and central pillar of the advent faith was the declaration, 'Unto two thousand and three hundred days; then shall the sanctuary be cleansed.' Daniel 8:14. These had been familiar words to all believers in the Lord's soon coming. By the lips of thousands was this prophecy joyfully repeated as the watchword of their faith. All felt that upon the events therein brought to view depended their brightest expectations and most cherished hopes. These prophetic days had been shown to terminate in the autumn of 1844. In common with the rest of the Christian world, Adventists then held that the earth, or some portion of it, was the sanctuary, and that the cleansing of the sanctuary was the purification of the earth by the fires of the last great day. This they understood would take place at the second coming of Christ. Hence the conclusion that Christ would return to the earth in 1844. But the appointed time came, and the Lord did not appear. The believers knew that God's word could not fail; their interpretation of the prophecy must be at fault; but where was the mistake? Many rashly cut the knot of difficulty by denying that the 2300 days ended in 1844. No reason could be given for this position, except that Christ had not come at the time of

expectation. They argued that if the prophetic days had ended in 1844, Christ would then have come to cleanse the sanctuary by the purification of the earth by fire; and that since He had not come, the days could not have ended.

To accept this conclusion was to renounce the former reckoning of the prophetic periods, and involve the whole question in confusion. It was a deliberate surrender of positions which had been reached through earnest, prayerful study of the Scriptures, by minds enlightened by the Spirit of God, and hearts burning with its living power; positions which had withstood the most searching criticism and the most bitter opposition of popular religionists and worldly-wise men, and which had stood firm against the combined forces of learning and eloquence, and the taunts and revilings alike of the honorable and the base. And all this sacrifice was made in order to maintain the theory that the earth is the sanctuary. God had led His people in the great Advent movement, His power and glory had attended the work, and He would not permit it to end in darkness and disappointment, to be reproached as a false and fanatical excitement. He would not leave His word involved in doubt and uncertainty. Though the majority of Adventists abandoned their former reckoning of the prophetic periods, and consequently denied the correctness of the movement based thereon, a few were unwilling to renounce points of faith and experience that were sustained by the Scriptures and by the special witness of the Spirit of God. They believed that they had adopted sound principles of interpretation in their study of the Scriptures, and that it was their duty to hold fast the truths already gained, and to still pursue the same course of Biblical research. With earnest prayer they reviewed their position, and studied the Scriptures to discover their mistake. As they could see no error in their explanation of the prophetic periods, they were led to examine more closely the subject of the sanctuary" (*Cosmic Conflict*, Ellen G. White, ch. 18).

[234] "They serve at a sanctuary that is a copy and shadow of what is in heaven" (Heb. 8:5 NIV).

[235] "After this I looked and in heaven the temple, that is, the tabernacle of the Testimony, was opened. Out of the temple came the seven angels with the seven plagues" (Rev. 15:5–6 NIV).

[236] (*William Miller and the Advent Crisis*, p. 159).

[237] (*Early Writings*, pp. 58 and 64, respectively).

[238] (*Apocalypse Delayed*, 1997, M. James Penton, University of Toronto Press, p. 18).

[239] "Moses was forty years in coming to the point where he offered himself to Israel... until the period which the Scriptures show us marked his second coming (October, 1874)" (*Watchtower*, Dec. 1, 1901).

[240] "In view of this strong Bible evidence concerning the Times of the Gentiles, we consider it an established truth that the final end of the kingdoms of this world, and the full establishment of the kingdom of God, will be accomplished near the end of A.D. 1915" (*The Time Is at Hand*, 1915 edition, p. 99).

[241] (*Watchtower*, 1881)

[242] "The Battle of Armageddon, to which this war is leading, will be a great contest between right and wrong, and will signify the complete and everlasting overthrow of the wrong, and the permanent establishment of Messiah's righteous kingdom" (*Watchtower Reprints, VI*, April 1, 1915, p. 5659).

[243] *Studies in the Scriptures*, Vol. 7, "The Finished Mystery," p. 128

[244] *The Watchtower*, Mar. 1, 1922

[245] *The Watchtower*, Jan. 1, 1924

[246] *The Time Is at Hand*; 1889, 1915 ed., p. 236

[247] "Christ returned and began ruling in the midst of his enemies in the year 1914" ("You Can Live Forever in Paradise on Earth," Watch Tower Bible and Tract Society 1982).

[248] *Watchtower*, Nov. 15, 1935, p. 331.

[249] "Eight years from the Autumn of 1967 would bring us to the Autumn of 1975, fully 6,000 years into God's seventh day, his rest day" (*Watchtower*, May 1, 1968, p. 271).

[250] "We are already living in the seventh millennium—since October 1872," (*The Time Is at Hand*; 1889, p. 363, 1915 ed.).

[251] "The Bible chronology herein presented shows that the six great 1000 year days beginning with Adam are ended, and that the great 7th Day, the 1000 years of Christ's Reign, began in 1873," (*The Time Is at Hand*; 1889; Foreword, p. 2, 1916 ed.).

[252] *The Truth Shall Make You Free*, 1943 edition.

[253] "In this twentieth century an independent study has been carried on that does not blindly follow some traditional chronological calculations of Christendom, and the published time table resulting from this independent study

gives the date of man's creation as 4026 B.C.E. According to this trustworthy Bible chronology, six thousand years from man's creation will end in 1975, and the seventh period of a thousand years of human history will begin in the fall of 1975 C.E." (*Life Everlasting in Freedom of the Sons of God*, President Frederick Franz, Watchtower publication, 1966).

[254] *Kingdom Ministry*, May 1974, p. 3.

[255] Watchtower Dates:

- 1844
- Miller's "end of the world." To Russell, start of thirty-year "tarrying time," corresponding to thirty years from Jesus' birth to his baptism. Abandoned in 1930.
- 1846
  End of the 2,300 days, George Storrs and others abandoned false doctrines, "sanctuary cleansed." Abandoned in 1930.
- 1873
  Six thousand years of human existence end, start of seventh millennium: The millennium of Revelation; the Day of the Lord. (New chronology making 1975 the end of six thousand years was adopted in 1943, but 1975 was not made an official prophetic date until 1966, with *Life Everlasting*.)
  Abandoned in 1930.
- 1874
  The start of Christ's invisible presence. Russell's most important date. *Three Worlds*, p. 175, *Our Lord's Return*, p. 27. Russell taught that this year marked the start of the Battle of Armageddon.
  Officially abandoned in 1943.
- 1875
  End of "Great Jubilee Cycle." End of 1,335 days in Dan. 12:12. The invisible resurrection of the saints began. (Please note that Russell taught that the "Biblical year" 1875 actually started in Oct 1874.) *Three Worlds*, p. 108.
- 1878
  End of gospel age, the rapture of the saints. *Three Worlds*, p. 68; *Proclaimers*, p. 632; *Divine Purpose*, p. 19.
  Abandoned after 1878.

- 1878
  
  Heavenly resurrection of dead saints. God's favor returning to the Jews. Kingdom of God started to exercise power. *WT*, Oct. 1879 [repr., p. 39]. *Millions* (1920), p. 27–8.
  
  Abandoned in 1930.

- 1881
  
  Rapture of the saints, including Russell and other Bible Students. *WT*, Jan. 1881 [repr., p. 180], Dec. 1880 [repr., p. 172], compare May 1881 [repr., p. 224].
  
  Abandoned after 1881

- 1910
  
  Expected rapture of the Saints.
  
  Abandoned after 1910.

- 1914
  
  The end of this world, Christ's literal return, the end of Armageddon, and latest possible date for rapture.

- Abandoned after 1914.

- 1914
  
  Christ's invisible return, start of reign as King, end of last days (earlier held to be 1874).

- 1915
  
  The end of the world. 1915 replaced 1914 in Russell's writings.

- 1918
  
  Fall of Babylon—"all false religion." See *Revelation Climax*, p. 260, which says, "So by 1919 Babylon the Great had fallen."

- 1919
  
  The Bible Student/Watchtower movement chosen by Christ to be only "channel" of communication from God to men.
  
  Current Watchtower doctrine.

- 1920
  
  Worldwide anarchy, collapse and fall of all earthly governments.
  
  Abandoned after 1920.

- 1925
  
  The end of the world immediately following the resurrection of "men of old" (Biblical heroes listed in Hebrews chapter 11). Establishment of Kingdom in Palestine. *Millions*, p. 88, 97. Very definite statements in *WT*, 6/15, 1922; 4/1, 1923, elsewhere.
  
  Abandoned after 1925.

# End Notes

- 1941

    WWII was expected to end in Armageddon, God's War. *WT*, 9/15, 1941, p. 288, talked about the "remaining months before Armageddon." Abandoned in 1943, after death of Rutherford.

- 1951

    This was thirty-seven years after 1914, like Jerusalem was destroyed in A.D. 70, which was thirty-seven years after Christ's death (*WT'S* chronology). Some *WT* articles in 1950 hinted strongly to this parallel. *WT*, 11/1, 1950, p. 407; 9/1, 1950, p. 277; compare *WT*, 3/15, 1951, p. 179 and 4/1, 1951, p. 214, both pointing out that "we are 37 years into the 'time of the end' of this world."

    Idea was abandoned in *WT*, 9/1, 1952, p. 542.

- 1975

    End of six thousand year of human history after WTS chronology. Strongly hinted to be end of the world; could only be a matter of "days and months, not years" before Armageddon. *Life Everlasting*, pp. 26–30; *WT*, 7/15, 1967, pp. 446–7; 8/15, 1968, p. 499; 5/1, 1975, p. 285. See also YB, 1980, pp. 30–31.

    Abandoned after 1975.

Chapter 18
Through the Door and into His Image

[256] 1 John 4:8 NIV

[257] Rom. 3:23 NIV

[258] "In him we have redemption through his blood, the forgiveness of sins, in accordance with the riches of God's grace" (Eph. 1:7 NIV).

[259] "I gave you milk, not solid food, for you were not yet ready for it" (1 Cor. 3:2 NIV).

[260] If we have sown spiritual seed among you . . ." (1 Cor. 9:11 NIV).

[261] "I planted the seed, Apollos watered it, but God made it grow" (1 Cor. 3:6 NIV).

[262] "By calling this covenant 'new,' he has made the first one obsolete" (Heb. 8:13 NIV).

[263] Ps. 103:12 NIV

[264] 2 Cor. 5:10–11 NIV

[265] 1 John 4:18 NIV

[266] "For this reason Christ is the mediator of a new covenant, that those who are called may receive the promised eternal inheritance" (Heb. 9:15 NIV).

[267] Isa. 53:3 NIV
[268] Heb. 5:8 NIV
[269] Heb. 9:14 NIV
[270] "Whoever would love life and see good days must keep his tongue from evil and his lips from deceitful speech. He must turn from evil and do good; he must seek peace and pursue it. For the eyes of the Lord are on the righteous and his ears are attentive to their prayer, but the face of the Lord is against those who do evil." (1 Peter 3:10–12 NIV).

To order additional copies of this title call:
1-877-421-READ (7323)
or please visit our web site at
www.pleasantwordbooks.com

Printed in the United States
104727LV00002B/181-183/A